# THIS
# WOMAN

*Being Authentically You, Driven and
Always Winning*

**Michelle Margaret Marques**

# DISCLAIMER

Michelle Margaret Marques, in her memoir *This Woman*, does, not apologise for anything. She writes the book with love in her heart and takes responsibility for everything she needs too. The chapters in this book reflect carefully chosen parts of her own story and the lessons she has learned along the way. The advice in the book is based on her views and represent how she healed and developed herself. Michelle accepts no responsibility or liability whatsoever on behalf of the consumer or reader of this material. She also does not suggest you should follow her advice or guarantee specific results for you. Any negative perception of anyone is entirely unintentional. Michelle cannot be held responsible for the use of the information provided.

*This is a book of memory, and memory has a way of telling its own story. I have done my best to make it tell a truthful story.*

*Each chapter in this book is the author's present recollections of experiences over a lifetime. Some of the names and characteristics have been changed to protect the identity and privacy of their families. Some events have been compressed, and all dialogue is given from recollection only.*

**ISBN:** 9781686830952

**Imprint:** Independently published

Connect to a safe space with Michelle at www.michellemargaretmarques.com

# CONTENTS

# FOREWORD

## BY NANCY FLORENCE

Look at This Woman!

Look closely...and you'll see Yourself.

This Woman is a modern tale of the most powerful cornerstones of a woman's life.

Michelle left no stones unturned.

She covers abuse, loss, life, death and everything in between.

You will nod a lot, have tears come to your eyes...and at times you'll find yourself smiling softly.

Michelle meant every single word she wrote in this book.

She is one of the bravest women I know, and I've learnt so much from her.

And by the way...(this is for you...the reader) when she tells you that she loves you...she truly means it.

She wrote this book for you.

So make yourself comfy and soak in all of the love that is infused in this book.

You'll be reminded that you are not alone.

Whatever you are going through, she has been through it, or a version of it.

Michelle has all the scars on her back and yet; she is a beautiful example of Joy and Femininity for all of us.

This book will help you get your Innocence back.

Michelle is one of the rare human beings on the planet who has maintained a child-like innocence and happiness.

She has been through hell and back, but she still loves herself, and she loves people.

In fact...she loves YOU.

Nancy Florence

Life & Business Coach

# THIS WOMAN

## INTRODUCTION

I am Michelle Margaret Marques, born Michelle Moffat in Glasgow to Scottish parents Margaret and Joseph. I grew up on a Glasgow council estate and although it wasn't easy and we didn't have a lot of money. We were surrounded by a large and very loving family who were fiercely loyal to each other (for the most part anyway). Oh, they could be just as cruel to each other as loving and loyal. However, the love and devotion always outweighed any other aspect.

My Mother came from a catholic background and my Father a protestant background. It wasn't easy growing up with that mixture of backgrounds in Glasgow, and I was often beaten up by both sides, just for being who I was. I was taught that I should never back down, I should never show fear, and I most certainly should always stand up for myself and stand my ground even if my head was being kicked in, and I did, and I still do. I grew up strong and no matter how horrible it may sound or seem to have been. Although I didn't know it then or could I have ever even begun to understand. My childhood taught me every lesson I ever needed to

3

build the life I was destined for. A destiny that is far more important than the turbulence I endured. I attribute that background to the iron backbone and sheer resilience I pride myself on having now.

A champion cannot help do what they were meant to do, it's the drive to do what I'm good at. Despite the turbulence of my journey, I believe I have lived on course to a life I felt drawn to. A life that has driven me to fully engage in my purpose, a life that only I could uniquely accomplish.

I believe I was given a predestined purpose, a drive for the contentment of a life well lived and the rewarding task of acting in my gifts. A life that had run its course.

Throughout this book, I am going to take you on a journey of handpicked pieces of my life, those pieces will give you a complete insight into the woman I am today and how I got there. How and why I never gave up, why I live with fierce authenticity and take full responsibility for my part in it all. Why I do what I do, live with fire in my hair while I'm doing it all. And how you can do it for yourself too. (Without a considerable chunk of the turbulence and heartache I've endured)

Warning some parts of this story are graphic and will shock you. My intention here is to be raw and authentic and at no point have, they been included for the sake of the story or cause shock and awe.

You may feel emotional, and I hope that you allow yourself to feel that emotion and embrace this journey with me. I fully intend that this journey awakens the champion in You too.

My intention throughout this book is to really stir your emotions, and I know we will laugh out loud, wonder what the fuck I was sometimes doing, gasp in shock, get angry, feel sad, sob uncontrollably if you are anything like me that is, giggle and be inspired all in good measure. My wish is that you embrace this journey with me fully and completely. Let it resonate with the parts of you that it needs to resonate with and let go of the elements that it do esn't and just enjoy the bloody ride in between. It does get messy at times, and

I suggest you find yourself a big cosy chair in a quiet space, trust me you won't want to be disturbed. Have some tissues, some chocolate and possibly some really great wine to hand when you sit down to read. And please please please above all else let it awaken the champion in you.

# CHAPTER 1

## MY SEXUAL ABUSE

### THE LITTLE GIRL THAT HAS NEVER GIVEN UP FIGHTING!

This story began in 1984. I was ten years of age, and I was sexually abused by my cousins' grandfather, who lived in the block of flats next to ours.

I was coming home from school for lunch one day, which is something I didn't often do and therefore, my Mother was not expecting me. Mr Aganue, my cousins' grandfather, shouted to me from his window and asked if I would run to the shop for him. I agreed and made my way up to the third floor to go get the money and find out what he wanted. When I arrived upstairs, his door was slightly open, and despite knocking, he didn't answer at first, so I opened the door a little and called out for him. He called out telling me to come inside. I went inside, and when I did, he closed the front door and locked it behind me. I remember feeling slightly on edge about this but didn't really have time to think much more about it. I then noticed that there was newspaper all over the floor in the hallway, I found it strange but again didn't give it much more thought until after.

I don't quite remember how he approached me or what it was he said at; first. All I do remember is that after he locked the door, he was sat on a chair at the bottom of the hallway, then he pulled me over to him. He began touching me and saying I shouldn't be afraid, I was scared, I felt paralysed with fear. I didn't understand what was happening, and I could never begin to imagine what was going to happen next. He pulled me towards him and began to take down my tights and underwear. I do remember him saying how small I looked and how nice that was to him. He bent me over in front of him and spread my legs, he then began touching my vagina and spreading it open, he kept saying it looked adorable, and he liked it. He started putting his fingers inside my vagina and saying that it was tight and it felt perfect. He continued putting his fingers inside me for a while, making comments about how good it felt and how nice it looked. He then attempted to put his penis inside my vagina, and it wouldn't go inside. He kept trying and trying, and he wasn't happy that he just couldn't get it all the way inside, it was so painful, I was so afraid, and I was crying, he told me to be quiet and that he wanted to enjoy it. He tried and tried again and again, but it just wouldn't go inside.

He sat back on the chair pulled me to the floor and told me he wanted me to kneel in front of him on the newspaper, he got hold of the back of my head and grabbed my hair tight, pulled my head down and put his penis in my mouth. He then pulled my head up and down by my hair frantically and enraged I was gasping for breath, gagging and crying. He continued to do this until he ejaculated in my mouth. When he let go of me, I was gagging and spitting the sperm out. He kept telling me to make sure it went on the newspaper. He then pulled up my underwear and tights gently, told me it was our secret and I shouldn't tell anyone. Gave me 20 pence opened the door and told me I should go straight back to school because I was late and I would be in trouble. As I was walking out of the front door onto the veranda, he said to me remember don't tell anyone about this it's our secret, you will get in trouble.

Although my house was just in the next building, I ran back to school as quickly as possible, trying to forget what had just happened, let alone make sense of it. I was so confused, I didn't know how I should feel, or what I should do. At first, I told myself to just forget it and that at least I could go get some sweets when school was finished with the money he had given me. Getting some sweets like that was a bit of a luxury. And I guess that was the only way I could try to deal with what had happened because I couldn't even begin to understand it. I didn't understand any of it and certainly didn't know how to start to understand it. So I did the only thing I could understand, and that was to pretend it never happened and focus on getting sweets.

Sure that was ok, to begin with, but something inside me just felt sick, and I kept spitting, I couldn't get rid of that taste in my mouth, all the way to school I kept spitting and spitting. No matter how hard I tried I couldn't forget it, and I couldn't stop the sick feeling or that taste in my mouth, even when school was finished, and I did go get those sweets. I went home and went to my room without having dinner, my Mother asked what was wrong, and I just told her I didn't feel well. This of course was very true, I felt all kinds of unwell but of course couldn't explain why to her, because at that time I didn't even understand why.

The next morning, no matter how hard I tried, I could not put this out of my mind. I could not stop feeling sick, his voice ringing in my mind telling me it was our secret, and I would get in trouble. But I knew inside something wasn't right, and something was telling me it was him that would be in trouble, not me. I was also feisty back then too, and there was never any trouble I didn't handle or was I afraid of. Remember I was taught to always stand up for myself and to never back down and at that time, I had an immensely loving and protective family. Especially my Grandmother, who absolutely adored me and I could go to for anything. We always had a voice in my family, sometimes we had to shout to be heard of course, but we always had a voice.

So instead of going to school, I went to my Grandmother who only lived on the next street. When she opened the door and saw me standing there, she immediately knew something was wrong. I didn't know how to tell her, and in truth, I don't remember what I said to her, I just blurted it out as best I could, looking to find some sort of answer or some understanding. My Grandmother held me and told me very gently; this was not my fault. I could never be in trouble for telling anyone and that she was glad I had the courage to never keep this a secret. At that point I stopped feeling so sick and stopped focussing on that taste in my mouth, although this would never be ok, I felt better at that moment, and I knew I had done precisely the right thing. In some ways, I'm glad that experience happened to me at a time in my life when I didn't fully understand the gravity of it. However, the severity was to take its effect later, and we will revisit this a bit further down the line.

My Grandmother handled this with such care and grace; actually, she told no one at first, and she and I went straight to the local police station. Her primary concern was to take care of me, with as little outside influence or fuss as possible. While at the same time having this officially logged as soon as possible. Had she told my family before the police picked him up, all hell would have broken loose and my uncles would have killed him.

I remember having to wait at the police station in the reception for a very long time, they didn't seem to take it that seriously at all. We were eventually taken into this very white room, with very stark lighting, it was not comfortable at all. I was interviewed with my Grandmother present, and I tried my best to answer the questions and give as much information as I could make sense of at that time. I didn't know how to explain some of the things that happened, I was ten, I didn't know how to describe what he had done or how it made me feel. It seemed like these questions went on forever and were repeated again and again. My Grandmother was frustrated and annoyed as it appeared yet again, they weren't taking it seriously. We waited a long time after the interview. I was then taken to another starkly, very brightly lit room where a doctor examined me and performed a vaginal examination. This was all too much for me and very confusing. This was another man putting his fingers inside me, and I was now being told this was ok. I was so traumatised by this that I don't remember much after the physical examination. However, I remember very clearly the doctor telling my Grandmother that although there were signs of vaginal interference. Because actual penetration didn't occur, there wasn't enough evidence to prove he had done this to me. As an adult, I'm appalled that he would take such a narrow-minded view and be so quick to conclude that there was not enough evidence. The police proceeded with charging him with sexual abuse, however, after a court hearing, they never gave him a custodial sentence.

After some time, I moved on and continued with my life, trying to put that behind me, and right at the point where I really thought I had forgotten it and in truth mostly I had. My cousin admitted to my Uncle that the sick individual had been abusing her for years. I was 17 when this happened. That haunted me from then on, and I felt responsible somehow. If I had done something sooner, there would be more evidence. If I had fought him at the time or screamed and screamed until someone heard, they would have caught him, I would have been taken seriously, and he would have never been able to do that to anyone again. He may have picked the wrong person when he picked me because I was never going to stay quiet, and he actually took a significant risk in doing so, but he picked me at the right time for him to still get away with it at that time. He chose the right person when he picked her because she was just the right kind of quiet and awkward. Always sat in the corner reading a book, everyone always thought she was just weird and kind of ignored her, although we understand now why she was the way she was. She came forward at precisely the right time for the law to take her very seriously. Plus, this was now the second report against him, and they had to take it seriously. I was also re-interviewed, and he was charged for both accounts of sexual abuse. A more significant trial started at that point, and we gave evidence via video link. The newspapers began reporting about it, and a couple of other women came forward who had lived in his building when they were younger. He was sent to prison, I can't remember the exact details, but I think it was a one year sentence reduced to a few months because he was in his 70's at that time. I remember walking down the street one day and suddenly freezing when I saw him walking towards me, he had been let go, and I didn't know, I will never forget how paralysed I felt in that moment, it was like being right back in that house. He actually died not very long after he was released from prison, which I remember at the time was a great relief to me, and I actually felt he had finally got what he deserved now.

My cousin and I had many conversations after that and the details we shared helped us both over time. I began to see that I did what I was meant to do, and I was not responsible for the authorities, not taking me more seriously. I remained faithful to the feisty person with fire in her hair that I am today even then and in fact, if I hadn't have come forward it may have been even worse for her, and they may not have taken her seriously either. Over the years, I've dealt with the trauma as an adult. I've even managed to forget a lot of the details of those conversations. However, there is one particular that will never leave me. My cousin told me she can't even put milk in tea because it reminds her of sperm, imagine what it was like for her feeding her baby day in day out.

It only happened to me once, and I am thankful that I had the strength to tell my Grandmother and that I knew I had a loving place where I had a voice. Despite this, for a long time, I even felt guilty that I had the strength to stop him ever coming near me again, and she didn't. I understand we are very different people, she wasn't as strong, and more to the point didn't have a voice or such a loving place to come forward in. Her side of the family was not as warm, in fact, I am utterly convinced on some level they knew what was happening, but that's not part of my story.

I thank myself for being the strong person I am and have come to understand that we are all responsible for ourselves when the day begins and ends.

Although I suffered a lot through that ordeal and beyond the suffering, I put myself through later on was in some ways much worse and had far-reaching effects on my adult life. As I said earlier, I am glad I didn't really understand it at the time. However, later, when I had to relive it, and I could understand it. It became an even more significant trauma with much more severe and lasting results. In my relationships, I always felt insecure, I never felt really loved or safe. I always felt very uncomfortable about sex and conditioned myself to just put up with it. Go through the motions as it was a normal thing that happened between two consenting adults. Although I could rationalise why I felt that way, I could never let go and really enjoy it. It took years for me to deal with the after-effects of this coming back up in my adulthood and in some ways I relived it in every new relationship and intimate encounter I had, until I really truly unpicked it, realised that I needed to forgive the ten-year-old girl inside me that I thought had let me and everyone else down. I needed to let go of the thought that the feisty fighter had abandoned me right when that little girl needed her the most because she never abandoned me, she was right there protecting me all the way. I needed to make peace with what I did or didn't do in those moments where I blamed myself for allowing him to do that and understand that I probably did the very thing that kept me safer than I could have possibly been if I had put up a fight or screamed. I needed to learn to truly love myself and appreciate that I was still lovable. Finally, I needed to understand it for what it is, it's no better or worse than it is, it just is. It just forms part of my story, it's no longer part of me or takes up any power in my life. I am the only one responsible for giving it power, and I choose not to.

I feel it's essential to give you a sense of how much it took for me to write this, the sheer fear I felt sitting down to begin this chapter because I didn't really know what was going to come up and how I was going to feel about what might come up. How writing it made me feel at specific key points and the sense of relief and fearlessness I now feel having gotten to the end of that piece of my journey. Because as much as it is essential to tell the story. It is just as vital to give you a complete view of the emotions and a window into who I am and how I deal with the journey I have had early on in your journey through my life with me after all the title is This Woman (smiles and a little cheeky giggle). It's also important because I want to give you strength in knowing you can absolutely overcome the effects of anything if you look inside, genuinely love yourself, take power back for yourself and choose to see it as just part of the story.

When I began to write my fingers began to get cold, when I started to get into the details of what happened, I began to feel uneasy, my stomach began to churn. The more information poured out the sicker I felt, and at one point, I actually thought I needed to be physically sick. I wanted to stop writing at the same time I wanted to write more. I have known from the beginning that this chapter was going to be one of the hardest to write and in many ways, it has kept me from writing this book sooner. When I was giving the really raw and graphic details. I felt cold, physically in my body and psychologically in my mind. The systems way of dealing with it, I guess. Surprisingly I didn't cry during the details of the actual abuse, but then again it isn't really a surprise to me because I made a decision a long, long time ago never to give up any tears or power to that incident again, and once again my feisty fighter protected me just like she always does. No surprise there, I hear you say.

I did cry three times during this chapter, in fact, make that four now (there I go again, smile) and that was when I began to write about how gentle and caring my Grandmother was and how going to her made me feel better immediately. I also cried when I was talking about forgiving the ten-year-old girl inside, in many ways, I still carry her with me, but I chose to bring her courage and fierceness with me these days. I also cried when I began to explain how I felt a sense of fearlessness reaching the end of writing that piece of my journey, and I have to say I feel the same sense of fearlessness now having wrapped up chapter one.

# CHAPTER 2

## GIVING BIRTH AT 16

Yes, I know right, oh and I really thought things through before having sex for the first time. I had been dating my boyfriend since I was 14 and we planned everything properly, waited until my 16th birthday Oct 1989, and then had sex, 16 was the legal age in the UK, and it felt right to do it properly so to speak.

We used protection, and everything was fine, or so we thought. Except five weeks later, I found out I was pregnant. That was not part of the plan, oh no it really was not. I planned to go to business college the following January, I planned to have a career. At no point did I even consider the plan to include a baby.

I was freaking out when I found out, I was terrified. I thought my Mum would kill me for sure, I really didn't want to have to tell her. Somehow, from somewhere I summoned up enough courage to speak with her and to my surprise, she didn't kill me, obviously. She didn't shout or scream, she didn't cry, blame me, shame me or throw me out the front door. All of which I had imagined in my mind over and over again. No instead my Mum was the most amazing, understanding and surprisingly calm she could have ever been, she told me how disappointing that was for sure, but that didn't change the fact that she loved me and would support me 100%. This conversation with my Mum actually became one of the most amazing conversations I ever had with her. I still draw strength from it today and cherish every single word. If it hadn't have been for this one conversation and this incredible life-changing situation I found myself in, my life may have been very different. I owe a hell of a lot in my life to this conversation.

So you want to know what the conversation was right? Ok ok, I'll tell you all about it. My Mum told me this doesn't change anything you want to do with your life, it just alters the path, it may slow you down, but it won't stop you. You can do anything you put your mind to, you were meant for more, just because you were born in a council estate in Glasgow does not mean you were meant to stay there. Just because you don't come from a wealthy background does not mean you are expected to remain there, you were born for more than this, you are meant for bigger things, and you can do anything you want. I still remember every single word as if it was yesterday. I should have every word memorised because I have played that conversation over in my head thousands and thousands of times, and I draw strength from it each time life throws a curveball. I hear her voice as if she is in the room with me talking me out of whatever negative feeling or reaction I could choose to have and every single time just like I did when I was sixteen, I pick myself up and get on with it. Or get up, dress up and show up as I say now. My Mum also told me that she was pregnant with me when she was sixteen, and she didn't have the support of her family. She ran away with my father until I was born, and she didn't want the same negative experience for me. She had wanted to become a designer for wedding invitations and that having me changed that, she never did it, she also didn't want that for me. I feel so honoured that my Mum had learned so much from her experience. And come through life with the ability to have such care and support. Passing on her lessons and changing the outcome for me.

Her lesson to me may have been too late to prevent the history of teen pregnancy. However, it was the most life-changing lesson I have ever had in breaking the cycle of adverse outcomes. She said you will call the college tomorrow and explain, you will defer your start date for a year, you will have this baby and you will go to college. Said in a tone of voice I knew all too well, there was no argument to be had, (giggle). She said I will look after the baby while you go to college and I want you to enjoy it, go out with your friends and be a student. I know you have already guessed it, however, I can confirm that is exactly what happened. My Mum is my superhero. She took care of my son and gave me the kind of support I could have only ever dreamed of. It's because of her understanding, belief and support. I am the person I am today, not to mention I wouldn't even be alive without her.

I know you must have had some preconceptions going into this chapter. This was going to be another terrible story of a teenager who had an awful time being pregnant and giving birth, no family support as the usual story goes. Oh, don't get me wrong giving birth to my firstborn was no joke, 29 and a half hours in labour. My Mum was with me the whole time, she refused to let them give me an emergency c-section because my son's cord was around his neck, the labour was taking too long, and he was becoming distressed. She said no give it a while longer he can do it, and she was right. He was born 30 minutes or so later, he was blue, and it didn't seem like he was breathing, doctors all rushed in the room in frantic commotion not telling me what was happening I started to panic and think he was dead, then suddenly he let out this cry, he spent the night in the critical care unit but he was absolutely healthy. The midwife was not, so understanding about teen mothers let me tell you, she was borderline nasty to me in delivery. Before she left she actually said to me, I'll see you here next year and I said no, you will never see me again, but I digress.

Giving birth to my son didn't just change my life in many beautifully surprising ways and some tough ways too. It changed me as a person, it gave birth to my new life and made me even more driven for a better life than I had ever had before. Gave me the responsibility for another human being that relied on me for everything. Of course, at times it felt like way more responsibility than I wanted or could cope with, however, it made me absolutely determined to give him a good life and all the love I had inside me. It changed the course of my life forever, and I would honestly not go back and change one single thing, yes I mean it, I wouldn't change a thing. It too made me the person I am today, and I am so grateful the universe chose me to live that experience early on and the universe and my Mum knew I was just the right person for the challenge and the lessons. I'm even more grateful that I got to give my Mum the gift of a grandchild, the only grandchild she ever knew. If I hadn't gotten pregnant at sixteen, if I hadn't had the courage to see it through, if I hadn't have had my Mum's support, she wouldn't have had the joy of having a grandchild, she wouldn't have witnessed his birth, she wouldn't have shared that time and love with him and I wouldn't have gotten the most powerful lessons I have ever had, and you see now, my life may have turned out very differently. All because of two people, (my Mum and my son) my life became the most beautiful challenge of who I really was deep inside and no one can ever take that away.

My Mum died at the age of 37 when my son was just 26 months old, I am grateful the universe gave me the biggest challenge of my life so early, for her and for me. Those three years between me getting pregnant and my Mum passing away were the closest we ever were, and we shared so much during that time that I cherish, I am beyond grateful that I got to share such precious gifts and moments with her and all because I had a plan, or so I thought, (smile). It's hard to explain that those three years were some of the most challenging years of my life. Yet some of the most cherished and beautiful.

You will learn the full story about those years as we go through this book, however, just to give you some perspective on the magnitude of challenging and beautiful I will tell you this now. Pregnant at 16, gave birth to a healthy son just under three months before my 17th birthday, almost died when my son was six months old, my grandmother died two months before my 18th birthday, and my Mum died ten days before my 19th birthday. The most important women in my life now gone, a single mum with a 26-month-old son, a family that just absolutely fell apart and now I was on my own with no real support, no real love outside of my son.

Everything I knew at that point gone, my life changed again in another grand challenge. My superhero and biggest supporter has gone, just like that my world turned upside down. I had my Mum for such a short time, it felt like it was gone in a heartbeat. However short I had her in physical life, she is with me always and everything I ever needed from her she gave it to me, every bit of love, every lesson, every belief in who I am, she made sure I had it. I am more grateful for what she gave me than I can ever really express in words. I am devasted by her loss, and I wish she got to see my life grow and my other two sons, and my daughter. I wish, I could still share precious moments together, however, I know she's never really gone because she gave me everything I needed, I know she watches over me from my head to my toes, and she walks with me everywhere I go. I talk to her every day, and I know how deeply proud she would be.

I want you to know, no matter how tough, how painful, what the challenge or heartache maybe, you are enough, you will get through, you may or may not have someone giving you fantastic support or teaching you valuable lessons. Just know this, the universe sends you everything for a reason, you may have manifested it from negative thoughts or experiences, or you may have manifested it from positive thoughts and feelings. No matter how it came into existence in your life, it's yours to own, and you have one choice own it like the beautifully courageous person I know you are or let yourself be a victim of it. I know which one I choose, and I also know which one has the hardest road to travel. Ultimately the choice is always yours, chose wisely and be strong, I know which one you are going to choose, (smile)

I don't even know you yet, but I love you still.

# CHAPTER 3

## THE DAY I TOOK MY LIFE INTO MY OWN HANDS
### (Literally)

This day started just like any other. Except unbeknown to me, it was going to be one of the most life-defining days of my entire existence so far, and possibly still is many years later.

I woke up with my then six-month-old son needing a feed and a cuddle, a big smile greeted me, and we snuggled for a few minutes, before feeding, bathing and dressing. It was a lovely day, and that evening my son was sleeping over at my mother's, a rare chance for me to relax and get some rest, and for my mother to spoil her only grandchild at that time.

I just didn't know my evening was going to be anything but relaxing. However, I did get much more rest than I ever anticipated. This was the night I almost died at the hands of someone who was meant to love me. Someone who was meant to protect me, meant to be my best friend and the father of my son.

It began as a usual argument, he was angry that I would not comply with yet another demand from his mother and he hit me with a shoe, lots of things went through my mind in just a few seconds. I thought is this really going to be my life, is this really what I am going to accept, is this the life I want for my son, so many questions and every single answer was no, no-no-no. You see, this was not the first time he had been violent. No this was now the third time, and at that moment I decided it was going to be the last. No more chances, no more begging to come back, pleading and crying, manipulating and controlling. On his knees in tears, making me feel like the terrible one. Oh no, this was not going to be my reality anymore I had decided, and I was ready to stand up for myself. I knew I didn't deserve this, I knew I was worth more, and I definitely knew how to fight for myself. I know you have learned a little about me by now. And I know you know, my very being was a product of fighting for myself and standing up for myself. It had been woven into my DNA growing up, and I wasn't about to abandon that part of me now.

At that moment I made one of arguably the most stupid, non-rational decisions I've ever had to make ( I would say it was actually one of the best) I know, what the fuck is she talking about. Let me explain, I hit him back with the shoe, yes I know I hear you screaming what the fuck, I could have done a whole host of other things, like walk out, call the police, lock myself in another room, go to a neighbour, go to my mother's, many things I could have done right? And that was the action I decided to take, remember I am a fighter. At that moment that was the right decision for me, and I actually take responsibility for my part in what I am going to tell you happened next, and I still stand by this being the right decision for me today and I say with the utmost conviction the right choice for me! I do not advocate this as the right decision for anyone else in the same situation. However, I had to stand up for myself; it was what I needed to do to break this cycle. In my whole life, I had never let anyone beat me, and I had to stop it right there and then.

So now I am done justifying the ass off of my decision (smile, giggles) let me get on with the story.

After I hit him back with the shoe, remember that far back. He hit me with a glass bottle, knocked me to the floor and began kicking me and kicking, and kicking, and kicking. So much kicking I could fill a page, but I won't put you through that. All I could do was curl up in a ball and try to protect myself as much as possible. I laid there while I was violently assaulted by the person who was meant to love me the most, thinking about my beautiful six-month-old son thankful he wasn't there, (this time) and hoping I would actually see him again let alone cuddle him. I want to reiterate that to you, because if you have or are experiencing violence in your relationship. I want this to resonate with you deeply, that person DOES NOT LOVE YOU, and YOU DESERVE A MILLION TIMES MORE. Please hear this loud and clear the caps are for a reason, if I could, I would literally shout that at you, and I'm serious.

He kicked me until he ran out of energy or anger, I suspect both. He then left me there on the floor and left the house. He had no idea if I was dead, alive, or dying, but he just left me anyway. This person DID NOT LOVE ME, he didn't even care enough to get help, make an anonymous call or take any action at all, he just disappeared into the night. I was left unconscious, and I don't quite remember, but I guess I was pretty much unconscious all night. Thankfully my next-door neighbour came knocking on the door the next morning. After hearing all of the shoutings and screaming the night before she knew something was wrong, she made her husband kick the door in, and they found me on the floor. Called an ambulance and my mother was told that due to internal bleeding, I could have died if I hadn't gotten to the hospital in time. They estimated I had 1 hour to live when I was brought in. I spent weeks fighting for my life, now I was a fighter for real, and thankfully, I still am. I was left with, broken and cracked ribs, a dislocated hip, bust up face and body and couldn't walk properly.

The good news, I recovered fully, and I never took him back, I never gave space for the crying and begging again, I never spoke to him again until my son was 10 years of age. I broke the cycle, I won the biggest fight of my life, I put myself through hell, but I came out the other side victorious and stronger, and I actually thank myself for having the courage to make the decision I made, I knew it would result in him beating me, of course, I didn't think he would beat the shit out of me and I would almost die. I couldn't have predicted that, however, what I absolutely knew would result from any kind of severe action he took was that I was definitely done with the relationship and wouldn't go back on that decision. I also knew that my family would definitely know about it, I would not be able to hide this like I had hidden the other two assaults. You see what was arguably the most stupendously crazy thing I have ever done was, in many ways in the most dramatic way possible I literally took my life in my own hands that day and I stand once again with the conviction that it was indeed one of the best decisions I ever made (arguably) giggle.

The lesson, no one on this planet has the right to even put their finger on your shoulder, and I don't care what you said or did. No one should ever accept or endure one moment of violence, especially and I really mean especially, from someone who claims to love you. I know you don't want me shouting in caps again, smile. If you take one thing from this chapter, even if you have never experienced violence, I hope the fact that you are a human who deserves to be treated with love and respect always resonates with you. Please, please know this, you are beautiful, you are worthy of love, you are lovable, and you are enough. Never, ever, accept any less than you want or deserve from anyone, no matter how much they profess to love you. Love is shown in actions of care, respect and kindness, anything other than that is NOT ACCEPTABLE. I know I'm doing the caps shouty thing again, I just want you to get it.

I may seem like I'm this badass warrioress (which I am, giggle) I want you to know it took me a long time to understand deep down I am beautiful, I am worthy, I am loveable, and I am enough. Even after standing up for myself, even after winning the biggest fight of my life and by the biggest fight of my life, I mean coming out of the other side, alive, sain, strong, loving, kind, courageous, full of passion and purpose. It took me a long, long time to know I am loveable and worthy, a long time to accept responsibility for my actions that night and to stop being a victim of what happened. What happened is now just part of my story, and I use it as fuel to thrive. I took my power back that night. However, I didn't really claim my power as my own until many years later, and I don't want that for you!

Whatever it might be that is causing you pain, whatever is causing you to accept a victim state of mind or situation, claim it now, take your power, flip your hair back and walk away into owning your life and your decisions.

I don't know you, but I love you still. Own it all NOW, smile.

# CHAPTER 4

## MY NANA SLIPPED AWAY.

August 1991, my grandmother (Nana) passed away peacefully in her sleep, after a six month battle with cancer. That battle was incredibly difficult for me, my grandmother was an amazing woman and a massive influence on my life, she also taught me I could have everything I wanted because she often gave it to me. (giggle)

I have to tell you that I actually stopped going to visit her a couple of months before she died and for a long time I didn't like admitting that to myself let alone the world. I was ashamed of those choices for a long time, and I deeply regretted missing out on those precious times. I didn't know at the time she was actually dying, she didn't want her grandchildren to know. In hindsight, had I known I would have spent every precious moment I could with her, but that was the point she wanted our lives to go on, as usual, she didn't want the fuss or to be a burden. She made her choice, and I had made mine. I didn't go to see her because of how sick she was. Skin and bone, I think at one point she weighed just over 60lbs, and she couldn't really speak. I just couldn't cope with the upset of it all and how it was affecting her, so I hid away from it and pretended it wasn't happening.

The day that she died, I was at work, and I just couldn't focus. I felt something was wrong, something deep down just didn't feel right, and as I searched inside for what the answer could be. I got a powerful feeling that I had to go see my Nana, this feeling hit me like a bolt of lightning, it was so intense I just knew without a shadow of a doubt I had to go, and I had to go now. I went into my bosses office and attempted to explain this less than a believable feeling, I didn't really understand myself let alone make sense of it for someone else. So I just blurted out, I have to go, I have to go now, I have this unexplainable feeling I have to go see my Nana, and I don't care if you fire me, I have to go now. I'm not sure if she was more shocked by my blabbering way of trying to ask her if I could leave work or if it was me blurting out I don't care if you fire me, she looked at me with shock and then said ok you go if you have to.

I got to my Nana's house as quickly as I could, I was expecting the worst by the time I got there because this feeling was so strong. When I got there, much to my relief and surprise, she was sat in the chair in the sitting room, looking better than she had done in months. She was talking fine, and we sat and chatted for hours, I sat on the floor in front of her while she brushed my hair, she always loved to do that, every chance she got she would have me sitting on the floor while she brushed my hair for 100 strokes, that was her secret method for healthy shiny hair apparently. I can tell you it was always more than 100 strokes, and I have a sneaky feeling it was her way of spending time chatting. Either way, I had great hair and a great bond with my Nana, win-win right. I told her how sorry I was that I hadn't been to see her. I had missed her so much, she told me it was ok, and I had nothing to be sorry for. I told her I loved her and although it didn't feel like it, nor could I have realised it at the time that was our last conversation and the last time she would ever brush my hair 100ish times. I didn't know it then, but that was our goodbye. Looking back now, it was the most beautiful goodbye, all wrapped in the added bliss of pure unknowing of what would follow.

For a long time, I thought about what I should have said that day, what I would have done differently. What I would have told her how I wouldn't have left to go home, I should have stayed longer. If I had known, it would have been so different, and of course, it would have, but not in the way I was trying to convince myself it would have. It was beautiful just the way it was, and it happened just the way it was meant to, and now I'm incredibly grateful for the sublime bliss of the unknown and for the joy of that afternoon, just sharing time with her in love and normality and when the end came that is precisely what she wanted.

I was back at home when there was a knock at the door, it was late now around 10 pm, and immediately I knew something was wrong, that intense feeling I had in the morning was soon back, and I rushed to get to the door, I opened the door and my uncle David was standing there. It was rare for him to visit, let alone at 10 pm so now my feeling was confirmed I knew without him saying a single word something was wrong. He came inside, and we all sat down with my Mum, and he broke the news, my Nana had passed away that evening, slipped away peacefully.

I had never experienced such overwhelm of emotions, thoughts and grief all at one time. At that moment, my life changed again, another challenge of who I was deep inside, another battle to overcome. My Nana was in my mind at that time, the most important woman in my world, and I really didn't know how I was ever going to get over her loss. I had gone through a lot up to then, but her loss was one I felt so deep I didn't think I could possibly survive it and I believe my Mum actually didn't. I will explain that later in the book.

I later came to realise she and my Mum were the two most important women of my entire life and they both gave me so much that I could never have gotten from anyone else. My Mum was never the same person again, a part of her died with my Nana, I think my Mum's heart was quite literally broken after the loss of her Mum. There had been until that day never one single day where she didn't see my Nana, the lessons of the past had taught them both, life was too precious to miss. My Mum and my Nana had missed out on valuable time before when my Mum was pregnant with me and just as I had somehow known to go see my Nana that day. My Nana was there the day I was born, sitting by my Mum's bedside when she woke up from an emergency c-section and my Mum never knew how my Nana knew to be there. The connection and bond I experienced with both my Nana and my Mum, is incredible and I really would have given anything to have had it for so much longer in the physical life. However, I still carry the strength of those bonds, and I always will. The love, the lessons and the relationship they shared with me and showed me how to have, enables me to share that with my children, my friends and my clients, it is quite simply what gives me the capacity to share so much of myself and it makes me an incredible coach.

Pay attention to the bonds you have in your life and the love you share. Life isn't always perfect, life sure as hell isn't always easy, but you can choose how you survive it all. You can choose the moments you cherish as beautiful and are meant to be and help you thrive. Or you can select the same moments to be painful and let them destroy you one moment at a time.

Choose life, live life, be joyful and live in love and cherish every single moment you have on this planet with every person you love or have loved. Although they won't always be there in your physical life, the memories, the moments, the bonds and the love will always be with you, that I can guarantee. I have lived through more death and pain over the years that it almost doesn't seem real. Sometimes when I look at my story, it seems like more than anyone could endure in two lifetimes, and people I know have asked how I am still sane (who knows if I am)  how I'm still standing and how I can always give so much of myself to others. My answer, because I can, I can do anything I put my mind to, and I do. I give because I can. I love because I can. I show up in this world the way I want because I can!

You can do it too.

I don't know you, but I love you still.

# CHAPTER 5

## MY MUM IS GONE

### But She Will Always Be With Me

My Mum died in 1992 ten days before my 19th birthday she is my hero and still the most significant influence on my life today, and always will be. You have already heard bits and pieces about my Mum, and I'm sure you are already beginning to understand why she is my hero; however, I want to tell you about who she was and why she will always be with me.

My Mum was one of the most beautiful human beings that ever walked this earth, she was a full beam of light and love. Always smiling and laughing, she had this big open smile warm and inviting, and she had such an infectious laugh. She had, love, for everyone and she would have done anything for you. She was always singing, oh my gosh music was such a big part of my childhood and still is a big part of my life today, wow she could sing. She would sing all the time, she played all kinds of music. Everything from country music to reggae, but Elvis was her favourite gee she had a love for him, just like half the female population back then. She listened to his music, and she watched every single movie, interview, concert, news report, you name it she would watch it, you get the picture right, she really liked his stuff (smile). The love of music and singing has been a big part of my family. My Papa (Grandfather) also had a fantastic voice and would always sing at family functions and get-togethers, no music he would just sing Ave Maria was his favourite and boy was it powerful. It's why I also sing, it lifts me up makes me feel alive and free, she also gave me that, and my sons and my daughter got that bug from me too. If you could hear us when we are all together in the car (giggle). I guess you could say it was passed down, he gave it to her (I'm sure someone gave it to him), she gave it to me, I gave it to my children, and hopefully, it will continue with my Grandchildren.

However, back to my Mum, she brought so much love, joy, support, encouragement and kindness to me, it still fills me up today. She was the most loving, big hugs, compassion and concern, she was also a great listener, and I went to her for everything I'm so grateful for having that kind of relationship with my Mum. I could talk to her about anything, good or bad, and she always had my back, but she would put me in my place if I were in the wrong. Both sides of her were equal in strength, her loving side and her authoritative side, either way, I always knew where I stood with her, and in the world, that's for sure, and she was still proud of me, so proud. Most importantly though I always knew I was loved unconditionally, and that is the most important gift any mother can give. She always helped with homework, asked about my day and my life and we sang danced and laughed all the time.

And as you already know the support and love, she gave me when I was pregnant and after my son was born, was above and beyond what anyone could ever have expected, or I could have ever asked for. Now the love she gave my son was so special. He was, her precious little bundle, she absolutely loved and adored him. She couldn't have loved him more, if she had loved him more, I think she would have popped. Every moment she could have him she did, he brought so much joy to her, and I am so grateful for that now, thankful she had that in her life. She wasn't just an amazing Mum; she was the most amazing human being ever.

As you know my son was just 26 months old when she died, she never got to see him grow and never got to meet my other children, I'm so glad she had that time with him.

My Mum died of heart failure, she was 37 years old, one day she was here and the next she was gone, just like that, missing from our life's. I believe my Mum actually died of a broken heart, as much as she had us and the joy we brought her, she never recovered from losing my Nana, that's my belief. She died exactly 14 months after my Nana, the same date of the month. My Nana 14th of August, my Mum on the 14th of October. It's a day I will never forget, the events that took place that day are etched into my mind.

It was early in the morning, I was getting ready for work, and there was a knock on my door, I thought it was the postman he actually had a habit of hand delivering my mail, for his own reasons. I was in a rush that morning and annoyed that he would knock on my door I remember thinking that bloody postman, I don't have time for him today, muttering to myself as I stomped down the hallway to the door. I opened the door forcefully in annoyance, and much to my surprise my Uncle Patrick and my Papa were actually standing there, now I knew something was wrong, everything inside me knew something was wrong but didn't want to believe it for a second. We try to make sense of it in our mind. My mind was racing trying to find a radical explanation. Why my Uncle and Papa were at my door so early, mainly since I lived about 50 miles away from them. They were wearing heavy rain jackets, and they would often go fishing at Loch Lomond which was right by where I was living, so my brain decided that must be it, they came to have a cup of tea before they went fishing. So I asked oh are you fishing at the

Loch and my Uncle said no we cam to see you, now my fears were confirmed something was definitely wrong. He said, let's go sit down. I need to tell you something. We went into my front room, and he sat me on the chair, and he kneeled down in front of me, my heart was racing just as it's racing now as I'm writing this. I began to shake, I knew something terrible was about to happen, he said to me your Mum died at 5 am this morning, I'll never forget those words, ever. I said how could you say such a thing, you can't say things like that and I got up and walked away, he got hold of me sat me back down and said she's gone, Michelle, I would never just say that to you, she died this morning, and I had to come and tell you. He then said, so we're going to go see her in the hospital, right. I'm going to take you to see her, right, come on, get ready and let's go. I remember I didn't cry, I went into my bedroom and stood there looking in my wardrobe for something to wear like it was a typical day, but at that point, it would never be an ordinary day again. We all got in the car, during the hour or so drive no one really said anything much. We went to the hospital and saw her, I still didn't cry, the doctor said he tried to revive her several times, and she just didn't respond. I thought, she just didn't want to come back, I was angry in a way, how could she leave me, leave my son, how could she leave us. I was numb, I can't explain the feeling of complete disbelief and shock, my mind just couldn't accept it, it was just trying desperately to adjust to this new reality. In fact, I didn't really cry for a few days, it didn't feel normal, I didn't feel normal. Later that day I went to the pub with my Uncle Patrick just the two of us.

We talked about her and shared each other's disbelief, we had a few drinks, and my Uncle said you are the closest thing I have to my sister now, I cry now writing this, but I didn't at the time. I cherish that time with my Uncle in those hours trying to accept that she was gone.

The last time I saw my Mum was just a day and a half before she died, my son was partially living with her at the time while I got myself on my feet after my father kicked me out of their house during an argument. We would get together on a Monday evening for dinner, and I would see my son. I wasn't feeling well that Monday, so I cancelled, she was so adamant that she wanted to see me and make sure I was ok that she made my father drive her out to see me, she didn't often make him do anything, let alone something he didn't want to, that's why I say she was so adamant, she must have wanted to see me very badly to make him do that and she wasn't an overly fussy person, meaning she didn't get all stressed out when we got ill, she just took care of us and gave us plenty of love and attention. She brought me some food and Lucozade, she always gave us that when we were ill, one of those crazy family remedies (we all have them) of course the other was a hot toddy, but that was only for when we were really ill. We sat on my bed and chatted, and when she was satisfied, I was actually ok she went home. Tears are streaming down my face right now, I didn't realise at that time just how significant that night was going to become in my life, just a Mum fussing over her daughter, but now it was much more than that. It was the last time I ever saw her, the last time I would ever speak to her, the last time she would ever hug me or tell me she loved me. As I reflect back on that night I wonder if deep down she knew she had to see me, just like I knew I had to see my Nana and over the years I've come to believe she did and I now realise that was her way yet again of making sure I knew I was always cared for and always loved. That's what she has still left me with, I always felt seen, I always felt heard, and I always felt loved and that is what I want to give to those I love.

That may have been the last time I saw my Mum or spoke with her in person, had a hug from her and the last time that she told me she loves me. However, it is certainly not the last time I felt her presence or her love, it's there every day. It isn't the last time I spoke with her, I talk to her every day, and it is definitely not the last time I heard her voice, I hear her voice each and every time I have a triumph, saying how proud she is, she always had so much pride for me. I hear her voice every time life throws me a curveball, telling me, you can do anything you put your mind to, this just changes your path it doesn't stop you, you were meant for more. I hear her voice in the music she loved, singing so beautiful and joyful, and I see her smiling and enjoying the music. I feel her warmth every time I hug someone, especially my children. I see her every time I look in the mirror, she's right there looking back at me, she's saying I love you, I'm so proud of you. I have her facial expressions, and I catch myself saying the same things she would say.

I have learned over my lifetime that there is beauty in everything, you just have to be open and willing to find it, sometimes you have to look hard, and I am grateful I have learned to do that, it took a long bloody time don't get me wrong and you have to go deep inside to find it, but it's there and believe me when I tell you it is in everything, even death, there is beauty in pain, but you have to heal the pain. The beautiful and yet painful thing about the loss of someone you love dearly, especially your Mum is that while the painful thing might be that they are no longer physically present in your life, the beauty is that they are in everything you do and everything you are. They are always around you, you will always have them within you, you will always carry their love everywhere you go, they will still influence you, and they are part of everything in your life. Cherish your moments and your love with those you love now, but remember they are still with you when they are gone.

I am incredibly grateful that I still hear her voice and her words of encouragement and belief. She gave me such strong and powerful messages every day, she gave me so much love, she had such beautiful faith in me and made sure she absolutely instilled in all in me, and it stays with me always. She is in so many ways why I am whom I am today, I live my life with the beauty she gave me and the sheer drive and belief she instilled in me. Both her loss and her influence in my life pushes me to become more every day, her words you were meant for more echo all around me, sometimes with, deafening sound when I need to hear it the most. She taught me to be me, thoroughly, and go after everything I want with everything I have inside. Some would say my life is lived for her, and my constant drive to become more is definitely for her. I would say my life is lived fully because of her and the magnitude of her loss makes me want to truly live the life she always knew was possible for me, her loss makes me want the most I could possibly want from life, people say life is short, but her loss taught me it really is. I want to live every inch of it, for both me because it makes me feel truly alive and for her because she didn't get to. Her beauty in my life and her loss inspire me to live life my way. A life I feel I was destined for, a life well-lived, a life with more experiences, in my years, a life where I lived a bloody good story. I live every day fully, and I grab it by the balls because she taught me I could, I do it for me, but I most definitely do it in honour of her. She wasn't with me long enough, but she gave me everything I ever needed to take me through this life in the time she was with me, she will always be with me.

I encourage you to focus on and work on it if you need to, bring the beauty with you in your life from each person that you have lost, and every other situation of pain, it is there believe me. Even in the worst times, there is still some beauty. You may have (had) the best Mum or you may not, chose to bring the beauty forward with you anyway, and if you can't do that, chose to bring the beauty of you forward with you, heal your pain and live in your harmony instead. Live life your way, with your love.

I want to share with you that this was one of my most painful chapters to write and in many ways, I kept putting it off. I sat down to conquer this chapter sever times, and the resistance defeated me until today. The opposition was still there today, and I almost did what I have done the other times, write something else or do something else just like we all do when we feel fear or resistance. Then I realised that if I didn't write it today, it was still going to be holding me back and denying me the feeling of really feeling free about sharing. I had to conquer the fear of feeling whatever was going to come up and get it done.

I gave you everything that was indeed inside me today. There were moments of sadness, moments of joy in remembering, especially the love she gave my son. There were times I had to stop, and I just sobbed, I don't mind sharing I sobbed hard at one point, but I didn't want to stop writing, I didn't feel I had to stop. I smiled, I laughed, and at times I didn't know what I was trying to say, but I wrote until it felt complete and I hope it inspires you to live the life you were destined for. Don't ever let anything hold you back, lean into it, feel all of it and fucking do it, do it with everything you have inside you.

I don't know you, yet, but I love you still.

# CHAPTER 6

## MY FAMILY BREAKDOWN

I am sure you would absolutely agree that the death of a Mother in any family has a massive impact. Every family deals with it in their own way, some better than others. I would honestly say that the families that deal with it well are the ones who are already close and have a strong enough bond. That wasn't the case in my family after my Mum passed away, our family literally broke down piece by piece. You see my Mum was the glue that held us all together, she was the reason we were a unit at all and, I can say that with a degree of confidence and certainty because we all fell apart after she was gone. The typical family I had grown up in ceased to exist overnight, and we now had sheer hell literally.

My father hit the bottle hard, my brother was running around, getting wasted and, my sister was also running wild. I had my son to take care of. We were dealing with each other full time again and the loss of my Mum in our own way. I can honestly say we all grieved independently of each other, we didn't grieve together, and we certainly didn't speak about how we felt or about my Mum. It was almost as if she was never there in the first place in some ways, yet there was a massive void at the same time. It's really fucked up and hard to get your head around if I'm bluntly honest and in a lot of ways that took more healing than the loss of her on in itself. I remember a newspaper article about my life, it was written because I had achieved a lot in the community. I talked about my Mum in that article, about her influence on my life and how amazing she was. It was a really great article, and you would think one in which my family would be happy ultimately. With my messed up family, oh no, not them. They were not pleased I had spoken about my Mum in a newspaper, anger was the feeling. My sister was livid and practically threatened to drag me all over the front garden at my fathers' house. She was screaming and shouting at me, how dare you speak about my Mum in the newspaper. Anyone would think I had said some terrible things the way she was reacting. These are the kind of fucked-up incidents I've had to deal with. There was always some kind of drama or argument. It's continuously draining and not a healthy environment to be in full stop, let alone conducive to healing a significant loss.

I could sit here and tell you a long list of horrible things this family has done to each other, violence, hatred, stealing, attempting to destroy each other in some way or other. My sister and I physically fighting each other, which resulted in me being rushed to the hospital with sliced feet, from knocking over glasses and standing in the glass while we were wrestling each other in a rage. So enraged I didn't even know I was standing in the broken glass barefoot. Gashes that narrowly missed my main nerve to my little toe. My father coming home from the pub, arguing with my sister and smashing plates, or putting his hand through my glass door. There was a lot of anger, a lot of pain, a lot of very unresolved grief, and we all took it out on each other in various ways. Some of us worse than others, although I never set out to cause hurt or heartache, I very much put all of my anger into whatever was thrown at me.

My boys grew up in this hell, and they were very affected by it. Especially Michael and when he became a father, he decided to take my granddaughter away and keep her away. I tried to get away, and we moved several times to keep our distance from the drama. It was never far enough, though, and it didn't seem to make a difference how far we moved, the tension always followed. I would run away, but I never cut my family out entirely, until years later, when I finally realised the only way I could have the life I really wanted was to cut them out. I had tried everything else up to that point, and it hadn't worked. I was always trying to make a better life, running my business and living in the right area. Making sure my boys went to a good school and travelling. Yet always felt I was being dragged backwards each step I took forward. The more I tried and achieved, the more drama that attracted from my family. It got to the point I was just drowning I finally had enough, and we moved down south. This was now far enough away to eventually be mainly out of the drama. Eventually, I cut them out completely.

You will be faced with choices for your own life, and to get what you really want for yourself. You will need to make some tough choices, and you may have to cut some people out of your life, including those that you grew up with. You are not responsible for the decisions of others or their behaviour. However, you are responsible for your choices and your behaviour. Take ownership of your actions and make the choices that are going to serve who you want to show up as in the world. Be bold and courageous enough to make the choices that will serve you and how you want your life to be. Don't ever allow anyone to infect your life with the level of negativity and pain that I have allowed. Don't ever allow, even the ones you love to have the far-reaching effects on you or more importantly, your own family that I accepted.

Be you, do you and don't accept anything less than the standard you want for yourself.

I don't know you, yet, but I love you still.

# CHAPTER 7

## A SERIES OF UNHEALTHY RELATIONSHIPS

And a whole world of pain and suffering, ultimately the same relationship over and over just a different person. Who was the common denominator? I, of course, and I take full responsibility for my part in it all. I still hadn't healed me, but the first step in that healing process was, of course, accepting responsibility for my part in it, owning it and not being a victim to it.

I was always a victim because guess what I made myself one. I attracted that into my life over and over again, until I healed and took back self. You have heard me talk a lot about taking back self, and that is one of the critical elements of healing along with taking ownership of your part in all of your suffering. Before I learned that I put myself through a whole lot of pain, some of which you have already learned about, let me tell you about my string of relationships, some just unhealthy and some extremely harmful. You will also notice a pattern, as I did and let me point out that the model gets better as I heal and take back self, with each experience I realise I grew and got clearer on what I wanted and what my standards are. You will also see it didn't happen quickly; they say the universe keeps teaching you the same lesson until you learn it. Well, it appears I was a slow learner back then (smile), but I hope by sharing my process, you can either avoid it or stop it much more quickly than I did.

You already know about the most extremely unhealthy relationship I was in, so no need to cover that again; however, it still forms the model. It's the very thing that instigates the pattern. After I promised myself, I would never be in an unhealthy relationship again, and no one would ever treat me like that again, I still did it. However, I'm going to throw a little curveball in here.

The next relationship I got into wasn't the unhealthy kind you will expect. We met after my Mum died and although I didn't realise it at the time. I was utterly broken, highly functioning but still broken. I was sending out an s.o.s. Subconsciously I needed someone to look after me. We attract what we want good or bad, I guarantee you of that. This situation was no different, I was drawn to him, not because I was physically attracted to him, but because he was a safe bet as I came to realise much later on. We don't always consciously make the connections at the time, and we often make choices without really understanding why we are doing it at that moment. He was kind, gentle, a bit of a nerd and didn't have very much experience with women, he was besotted with me and just absolutely out of his mind with pride to think I showed interest, and I liked that, I needed it. He was blind to the fact that I was almost broken or maybe he didn't care, he also attracted what he wanted, right. He was very loving, very giving, and I couldn't give it back. I got pregnant quite quickly, something his mother was absolutely against. He adored me, and he would have given me anything and done anything for me, and he did. I was now the taker in this relationship; he was filling up my cup so much and making it so fucking easy for me that I didn't have to give that much back. I couldn't give that much back, in any case, I didn't have the capacity to, I didn't have it inside to give. I needed to take because I didn't have any love for myself. I wanted affection from him when I wanted to have it, and when I didn't want it, I didn't want him anywhere near me, and I mean anywhere near me. I could have walked right over the top of him if I had wanted to and I probably did to some extent, except I had experienced that and I didn't want to be that person. I knew this relationship wasn't healthy for him or me, and I had told him so. I told him I wanted him to have the kind of love he felt for me with someone else, and I wanted to feel that kind of love for someone.

I wanted more, sounds crazy doesn't it, I had a man that adored me who gave me, everything and I wanted more. However, what I wanted was to feel more, I wanted to feel crazy love, crazy passion, crazy deep connection and no matter how much I tried and wanted to feel the same for him I just couldn't. He wasn't that person to me; he was my safe bet, the one that took care of me while I tried not to rebuild myself. Despite my honesty, he wouldn't accept it, we had my son Michael by that point, and he was determined to make it work. He was determined to show me he loved me and that we could be happy. Oh and he tried, he tried, the problem was the more he tried, the more I couldn't feel what I needed to and wanted to. An unhealthy place for us both and always feeling empty, I thought there was something wrong with me, I wasn't meant to be happy, I wasn't meant to have that happy family life. And I'm sure he felt insecure and empty like he wasn't enough and there was something wrong with him. Nine months went by after I had initially told him how I was feeling about the relationship. All that time, we were putting ourselves through pain, unhappiness and guilt before I finally got enough strength to end it. It was horrible, he begged me to keep trying, but I just knew I had to finish it for us both. He says I destroyed him, he moved away and didn't see his son, I found out years later that anyone new in his life didn't know he had a son. For a long time, I carried that guilt with me the thought of putting him through that much pain made me feel like a selfish person. Until I learned it was the best thing, the kindest thing for us both, we would have only destroyed each other.

Looking back I can honestly say, I had, love for him, and I was deeply grateful that he was there for me when I needed someone to look after me the most, but I wasn't in love with him, and I knew deep down it wasn't enough for him or me, and it wasn't fair on him or me. I know now, I got in that relationship because it was what I needed at the time and if I had met him when I was almost broken, I would have never even given it a second thought. I am grateful that I realised it was unhealthy and had the strength to end it for us both. My son was one year old at that time. I take ownership of my part in this, and I am glad I met him, I have no regrets. I was loved, and in many ways, I learned what love was, which ironically is what also taught me what I wanted to feel. I learned about myself, I healed a bit more, I grew and most of all I have a beautiful son from it.

My next relationship happened quite quickly after that, too fast and I can tell you what I learned, be careful what you wish for, remember the guarantee I gave you up there, yes you got it, it happened again. Remember I wanted crazy love, crazy passion and insane connection. Oh boy, did I get that? Remember I also told you that I got more precise about what I did want as I went through each experience, yeah I should have been clearer (smile), but I do get better as I go and you will too. Just don't do it my way please with the emphasis on don't (smile) Anyway, I digress. He was everything my previous partner wasn't, full of confidence, a bit of a bad boy (well when I say a bit) of course I later found out he was more than a bit. He drove a sports car (a sports car he then put upside down in a ditch) We instantly connected and we were together every moment we could be, he stayed at my place every single night.

He would go to work and come straight back to mine, it was full-on head over heels, couldn't get enough, crazy about each other and of course I know now that made me blind to the faults, the traits I should have avoided. We were just consumed by each other, and I got pregnant quite quickly, see another pattern (that one continues, smile) everything moved fast with us, way to fast even to think let alone notice he was the broken one this time. He would drink, way too much, but of course, I didn't see that. No, I was way too wrapped up in this little bubble of passion and love. We had a lot of passion, including when we would argue, and we started to disagree a lot after I got pregnant. I had a miscarriage, and as painful as that was, it brought us closer. We agreed we weren't going to have a baby now we were going to take our time a little more, the universe or my son had other ideas a few weeks later I found out I was pregnant again. What can I say (I told you it was passionate, giggle) The cracks just kept becoming more visible as time went on, he crashed his car, I was noticing just how much he drank, his father even harassed me about allowing him to drink so much. He was a grown man, a huge built 6"4 man, believe me, no one allowed him to do anything, he did what he wanted. I found out he was taking drugs when he went out with his friends (turns out he had always been taking them here and there) The abuse started, mental abuse at first, name-calling, putting me down, criticising how I looked, my weight. I would tell him I was going to end it if it didn't change, he would say who is going to want you, you are just a fat cow with three kids, no other man is going to want you. And for a time his abuse worked, I was back there again, wrapped in guilt for leaving my last partner, believing there was something wrong with me, I wasn't meant to be happy, I wasn't meant to have a happy family and I sure as hell wasn't important or loved. I began to believe relationships weren't for me, I just wasn't good at it, I wasn't meant to be in one, and I wasn't meant to be happy in one. I gained strength from that in a way, and I decided if I wasn't going to be in a happy relationship, I wasn't going to be in any. I knew I didn't deserve his abuse, and I knew I didn't want it for my sons or me. One night during an argument, he grabbed me by the hair, dragged me across the floor and spat in my face. She rose up, that fighter in me, there was no way in hell I was going through that again, not for a single minute. I picked the phone up called his mother, told her exactly what had happened and told her to come to get him and his things. She came straight away; she had already been telling me before this that as much as she loved her son, I deserved better and she was right. That was the end of that, right there and then. My son Michael went through hell after that breakup, he had come to see Liam's father as his own and actually called him dad by his personal choice, and as much as my ex welcomed that at the time, he didn't want it that way after the breakup. Stephen wasn't so affected; he hadn't ever bonded with him that much. He only wanted Liam; he was cruel. He would come to pick Liam up and wouldn't even acknowledge Michael (his way of hurting me) Michael would call out after him as he walked down the path to his car and he wouldn't look back. It was heartbreaking, Michael would be screaming I want my daddy, I want my daddy, I want my daddy. You have no idea what is like to sit and try to explain to a three and a half year old that isn't your daddy, and you can't go with him, the heartbreak is unbearable. I stopped him from coming to pick Liam up because it was just too painful for Michael. His mother would pick him up instead. Eventually, Michael stopped asking for him. I picked myself up, I lost a lot of weight, I started my own business, and I built my life with my sons on my own.

Deciding yet again I wasn't meant to be in a relationship, I was much better on my own, and now I had more evidence and a new belief to support that. It was safer to be by myself; no one could hurt my sons again; no one could hurt us again. There was no way they would get attached to someone, and no way someone was going to walk away from them and cause pain. Of course, I realise much further down the line I was probably protecting myself more than I was protecting them. I spent almost 13 years on my own raising my sons, that's how much protection I believed we all needed. I didn't want anyone else in their life, and I wanted their home to be safe. I wanted it to be their place of security, where they knew no one was going to hurt them or leave them again. Sure I dated here and there, but nothing serious, I didn't let anyone close enough, no one ever met my sons and no one ever came to my house.

Which also brought a series of unhealthy relationships, including being raped by someone who was meant to be my friend. And a couple of other attempted rapes too — casual relationships that were abusive or where I was being used in one way or another. However, my home was safe, and my boys had security. That was our safe space, and that's what mattered. During this time I also dated someone in New York, we were friends, to begin with, and actually, in a lot of ways he was my rock, he pushed me to achieve more with my business and be more assertive as a person, the quiet little girl from the UK he would call me (huh you a quiet little girl from the UK I hear you ask), he has had a lot of influence on who I am today. I loved him so much, but he didn't have the capacity to love me the same. As much as he was a rock for me, I could talk to him about everything, and he was emotionally supportive of what I wanted from my life, he wasn't emotionally available in any other way, he had his battle with trust, experience from his previous marriage.

I spent eight years trying to be everything I thought he wanted me to be, years of feeling insecure, trying to prove myself to him, show I wasn't like her, trying to get his love, his heart, and ultimately going through a rollercoaster of emotional turmoil, that eventually almost took my emotional wellbeing from me. The relationship, on the one hand, was a great support system for me and on the other was emotionally draining, in reality, it was terrific, and it was unhealthy in equal measure. He cheated, and he told me, I forgave him, but it didn't matter. I never felt genuinely secure, and I never felt emotionally loved anyway, he would never say I love you, it was always that's why I love you or I have, love for you. Again there I was wondering what on earth I had to do to be happy in a relationship, to just be loved and have that fairytale ending. Despite this, his influence pushed me to be stronger, it forced me to be more confident, pushed me to be surer of who I was and what I brought to any relationship. He didn't put me down or try to abuse me; he told me to be who I was and do what I wanted to do. As I stepped more into whom I was becoming and taking back more of self, I stopped trying to prove myself to him; I stopped trying to prove myself to me. I began to realise there was nothing wrong with me after all, he just didn't have the capacity for me, my love, my strength, my passion and my drive, because it wasn't me that wasn't enough, he never believed or felt he was enough and I can say that because we remain friends even now and he has told me. I have come to realise that's why he pushed me so much, that was his way of showing love, that's what he had the capacity for, that made him feel valued and worthy of me. It took me almost a year to decide to end things, it was one of the hardest decisions I have made, I knew I was never going to get the relationship and the love I wanted, but I didn't want to lose my friend. Something else happened that ultimately made me end this relationship, and I wanted a baby, (yes I know) I wanted a baby girl. I kept having these images, visions, call them what you want, but to explain I kept seeing this baby girl, she was around two years old, big brown eyes and lot's of curly hair, I spoke to him about it, and I told him I think she's meant to be mine. He would say he wanted a baby but one day. One day when I thought and asked, we weren't getting any younger and we had already known each other for eight years. As I was getting stronger in myself, I was growing tired of the delaying tactics and lack of genuine commitment. Also, these images were now getting stronger and the feeling stronger too. Which was just as confusing to me that I wanted to have another baby let alone was having these crazy images, but it was real. A friend drew this little girl as I sat and explained what she looked like in my mind. In the picture, it was so evident that this was precisely the image I had been seeing. I ended our relationship and thankfully, at least for a time remained friends, although of course it was nothing like the friendship we had shared and I no longer told him everything.

Now to my last ever unhealthy relationship, I know you are thinking, how many could there be in one lifetime, how much turbulence and shit can one person have been stupid enough to put herself through. The last relationship I have to tell you about now, and it is the only previous unhealthy relationship I will ever have to explain in the future. I know you just felt a sigh of relief (phew we are almost at the end of the rollercoaster of emotions) In another chapter, I will tell you more about the lessons and the beauty of my marriage. For now, I will stick to the main reasons why it was so unhealthy and tell you that in many ways it was the most damaging and has had the most in-depth effect on me, both good and bad.

I met my daughter's father in August 2010 after I was starting to rebuild my life from other suffering as you will learn later. It began with a spark, and we soon became inseparable, I also got pregnant quite quickly (see the pattern again) we decided we would make a go of it and we moved in together, this was now the first time I was living with someone after almost 13 years and also the first time my sons Michael and Liam were now sharing me with someone and having to try to accept someone else's rules, it wasn't easy and neither my boys or him took to the adjustment kindly. Let's say there was a constant battle of ego and male dominance that went on between them, they didn't like each other, my husband was trying to assert dominance, and my boys were far from accepting, neither side behaved well, and I was in the middle. My marriage was very unhealthy, not because of physical abuse or even any real mental abuse; however, I felt emotionally tortured. There was no intimacy, no affection, barely any communication. I would try to talk to him, but he didn't want to listen, he would dismiss my emotion, roll his eyes and say oh this again and tell me I needed to draw a line in the sand and move on, or he would just completely ignore me oh and yes I do mean downright utterly just block me out, he would sit and look right through me. It didn't matter if I was calm, angry, crying, or anything he would ignore me. This emotional turmoil was slowly destroying my wellbeing. The anger I felt inside was eating me alive, and it was affecting everything else around me. However, I stayed, and I dealt with that for almost four years, we didn't even sleep in the same bed for the last two years. I kept telling him I was going to go if it didn't change, he would say you're hell-bent on leaving, he didn't care, he still didn't change anything. I asked to go to therapy, he refused. I cried myself to sleep at night.

I laid there wondering why I just wasn't good at relationships, why I kept ending up in unhealthy, unhappy relationships, what had I done that was so fucking wrong. I was torturing myself, trying to figure out why he was doing this, why would he put me through this. I went back to my dear friend, you know the one that I had inside who told me I wasn't meant for relationships, and this time I did have more than enough evidence that I was better on my own. I was happier, on my own, no one to bother me or try to control me. Finally, I had enough I knew if I stayed, I was going to lose myself, ultimately, and be emotionally broken. I wasn't going to allow that now, after everything I had come through, no, no way. This savage, this fighter inside me wasn't about to give up now, instead of attempting to figure out why he was doing this to me. I had grown enough to know I had to figure out why I was fucking doing this to myself. Why I was accepting this level of behaviour, why I didn't just love myself enough to put myself and my happiness first and then it hit me, that's what I needed to do. I asked him to leave and he wouldn't, so I found somewhere else to live, and I moved out with my baby girl. (oh and let me tease you with a little secret I know you are wondering). My daughter is the girl in my visions; she is the exact double of that picture. If you ever had any doubt that you can attract what you want, please consider my guarantee proved beyond any shadow of a doubt) You will learn more about that in another chapter (smile)

With each relationship, no matter how unhealthy, came the lessons, the beauty, the scars, the strengths, and the gifts I promise you that. I believe I attracted each one for many different reasons, but most of all, they all came to teach me my worth, my strength, my capacity to endure and love. To show me, I am unbreakable, and I deserve everything I ever wanted. I got everything I ever wanted, and I call them Stephen, Michael, Liam and Caragh, they are my heart, my life and my soul, and I would go through it ten times over to have them.

As I write this book, I can tell you it's been over four years since I left my last relationship, and in that time, I have done a lot of unpacking, a lot of healing, a lot of personal growth. I have continued to put myself first, and I always will. I am happier now than I have been in my entire life. I have learned all of the lessons I was meant to learn from unhealthy relationships. I can say that not just with strength, but with absolute certainty. I say that because I have now for the first time in my life stayed alone because I wanted to be alone. I wanted to do the work it would take to heal, to learn, to get clear on what I want from a relationship and what will and won't work for me as a whole in my life now. Or for the life and lifestyle, I'm building. I can now tell you I am thoroughly happy alone, I love my life, and I love myself unconditionally. My turning point came when I learned to fall deeply in love with myself and accept all of my edges and imperfections. I'm more confident than I have ever been, I am unbreakable. I have learned that no matter what I will always be ok, and no one can ever change who I am in my core. I am loveable, I am worthy, and you bet your fucking ass I am enough.

I'm sure you have seen distinct patterns in my many mistakes; however, I'm sure you can also see clear trends in my growth too. Each time I was getting stronger, each time learning more, each time valuing myself more, finding more worth, falling more in love with who I am and each time taking back a bit more self.

Take back self, love you, be you, do you and don't ever accept anything less than you are worth.

I don't know you, yet, but I love you still.

# CHAPTER 8

## MY PAPA PASSING

You haven't seen me describe any positive male role models in my life so far, and this may not seem like the place to do it. However, my Grandfather (Papa) was precisely that. Especially in later years after my Mum passing. He worked away a lot when I was growing up, but when he was around, he was a significant influence. The things that make me smile when I think of him was his booming voice and his great character. He was a disciplinarian a lot of the time and was very serious about teaching us right from wrong. My Papa was a stringent Catholic and had very high morals. He was a very proud man who always worked hard and always provided well for his family. He cared deeply about how he was viewed in the community and did not like any of his family being at the centre of questionable behaviour. He could be hard at times, but deep down, he was a softy.

At times, of course, I really disliked how hard he could be. I would say in some ways, I was scared to let him down or get in trouble. He really hated us speaking Glaswegian slang, and whenever he caught us, he would correct us and make us repeat it the proper way. It annoyed the hell out of me back then, now I am so thankful for it. It's mostly because of that influence that I can express myself in a way that is understandable to anyone and feel confident in any social setting.

After my Mum passed away, my Papa was practically the only constant in my life. He was always at the end of the phone, for advice or support. Whenever I went home to visit, I went back to his house. Up until he passed away, I went home as often as I could. I took him on holiday to Jamaica for his birthday one year, and he protested about me paying for it the entire time (giggle). I'm so thankful I could do that with him, I couldn't have known then he wouldn't be here much longer. I think it was two years after that he passed away. He had been feeling down and lonely for a while before he passed away, I'm sure he was still struggling with the loss of my Nana and my Mum. My Grandparents were together for a lot of years, over forty, I think. I also think he had been drinking a little too much whisky. He had come through a triple heart bypass, and he was dealing with diabetes. However, overall, he was in good health, he was as strong as a bloody ox. Nothing much could keep him under the weather for long that is for sure. And he looked great for his age, in his seventies and still not looking a day over sixty.

He passed away, one-night peacefully in his sleep. In the home and the bed, he had shared with my Nana, with her picture right beside him. It is my belief he decided he had been here enough and it was now time to go back to her. This was another significant loss for me, and for me, I had lost the last constant influence in my life. The grief hit me hard and in some ways sent me on a spiral of emotion. All my pain, three of the most significant people in my world now gone. I felt like I had no one left, no one there for me anymore. I was now very alone, I felt deeply lonely. His funeral was tough for me, and I didn't stay long at the wake. I went back home to my life to figure out how I was going to deal with having no directly significant people in my life.

I miss him so much, although the influence he had in my life will always be with me. I miss his loud voice and his big laugh. I miss him holding me to a high standard; however, it is a standard I hold myself to now so very well. Thank you, Papa, you and your strong influence on my life will always be remembered and appreciated dearly. Your constant presence will still be missing. I love you.

I don't know you, yet, but I love you still.

# CHAPTER 9

## NEVER HAVING FAMILY SUPPORT

### And How It Made Me Stronger

This will be a quick one, I just love busting through these lessons it took me a long, long time to process and learn from and give them to you in a nice kick-ass short one (Ha). This is a compelling one, and I want you to really take on board the lesson and the beauty in it, don't get all relaxed because it's short.

As you know by now, my family went through some tough shit, and it basically fell apart after my Mum's passing, so no need to run all through that stuff again. However, this isn't just about my immediate family; this is about pretty much my whole family. They never believed in my dreams, they never thought it was possible, not just that I couldn't do it, they just thought I was living in the land of the coo.coo, and it just wouldn't happen. They believed that a young woman from my background, with no real financial support, could even begin to achieve the kind of things I wanted and have done, comments were made such as, you have forgotten where you come from, you think you're better than what you are. They would actually try to talk me out of things I wanted to do, tell me it would never work, I should just get a job and be happy. It goes deeper than that, they would delight in anything that didn't work out, comments would be made such as oh she's fell off of her pedestal, fell flat on her face again.

When I got a lovely house and car, I was told you don't need a big home and a nice car or when I took my sons on holiday or bought them good things. I was told they don't need fancy holidays and great clothes they just need love. When I worked hard, I was told I shouldn't be working all the time I should be at home with my sons. These comments also influenced my sons, and they would sometimes have the same attitude. I was laughed at, slagged off, put down and pretty much became the joke that everyone talked about.

I spent a lot of years angry, hurting and trying to prove myself, it didn't matter if I did well or I didn't do well. The outcome was still the same with my family, I was just a big joke, who kept chasing this stupid dream. When I went from project to project, they accused me of scamming, if I travelled a lot they thought I was drug trafficking. When I had success, they would say it wouldn't last. Pretty soon I just stopped telling them what I was or wasn't doing, it didn't matter to them anyway, and it was less fodder for them to chew.

After some time, I stopped trying to prove myself to anyone, I learned there was only one person I needed to prove anything to, me. I had known from the start what I was capable of, and I had done enough proving to myself by now of what was possible. I learned to love myself, I loved myself enough to never give up. I stopped being angry, which was the best thing that was to come from learning; I had nothing to prove to anyone. Although it took quite a while longer and a lot more lessons I finally stopped hurting, the lesson I learned from the whole experience was that I was strong, stronger than I ever knew or any of my family gave me credit for, it taught me that I could endure anything in business and still thrive.

My family not supporting me and not believing in me, and at times being downright cruel hadn't broken me, in fact, it did quite the opposite it had given me ovaries of steel, an iron backbone and every tool I needed to survive every single success and setback I have ever had the pleasure of experiencing. Going through such a constant battle of self with my entire family watching for my demise has taken me to a place of inner strength that is entirely unbreakable, and I have managed to rise above it all and never quit. Quitting, as you know, is the only form of failure. Not one single one of my family has ever bought a product that I have sold or that I now make, they have never paid for treatments in my spa, they have never bought a ticket to an event, a workshop or even shared my social media. You don't need to worry about the outside world when you are constantly challenged by those within. The good thing that comes is sheer fearlessness, I can honestly say I never worry about launching anything because there is no criticism that I cannot handle now, in fact, I don't even factor it anymore. I've also learned that your tribe are out there and there are people in this world who will just support you and be there for you if you just put yourself out there.

My family say they are proud now, they say you have done what you always say you would, and we should have supported you. I suppose it's beautiful, but it's been a long time since I needed to hear it. And it feels good that there is no emotion to it anymore, it's very freeing.

Go out there and get yours, whatever it might be, don't let anyone discourage you no matter where you come from, you were meant for more. Go, find your tribe and just fucking love yourself enough to keep trying no matter how many times you have to, get up, dress up and fucking show up.

I don't know you, yet, but I love you still.

# CHAPTER 10

## COMMITTING FRAUD

A series of bad choices and mistakes set me on this path of what could be seen as self-destruction. However, it actually resulted in a huge turning point for me, which is one of the reasons I include it in this book.

Being a giver has always been part of me and who I am deep inside, but it didn't always bring good things in return to my life. I was often told that I had a big heart and I gave too much, I gave to the detriment of myself a lot of the time. I'm sure you have also seen this in your own life. My heart would go out to anyone who was down on their luck or needed someone and immediately I would be whatever they needed, friend, advisor, helper, giver of anything they needed, I just gave, and I gave, and I gave, I gave without boundaries, I gave like a river without a dam. Until this situation taught me to build a dam, I still provide, but I give with a great big intelligent and incredibly well-designed barrier. It's quite the masterpiece the heart of the river is open entirely and gentle, but it has a very sophisticated filtration system, it keeps my river flowing fast and in the right direction. Or as Danielle Laporte would say, open gentle heart, big fucking fence.

Ok, now back to a series of some of the worst decisions I've ever made. It was around early 2006 when this story begins. My brother was in prison, ironically enough. During a visit, he told me about this friend of his who was also in the same prison. He told me how this person didn't have anyone to come to visit him or write to him, he was going to be in there for a very long time. My brother said I know how much you love to help people, would you write to him and maybe come visit him once in a while. Me being me, I agreed, the me I was then jumped at the chance to help this lonely person whom my brother seemed to think was a charming person. So we began writing, and I went to see him a couple of times before too long we had really struck up a friendship and I will go as far as saying I really became very fond of this person. He began relying on me for everything he needed, his uncle, or at least that's what I was told would put money in my bank account, and I would buy him what he needed. He would often ask me to keep some money for myself to use to cover my expenses of going to see him and getting his things. Everything was great as far as I was concerned, this was a sweet friendship, and I wasn't being taken for granted for once.

Only I'm sure you can already guess that's not where the story ends. He began to be a bit more demanding, and he wanted other people to put money in my bank account, claimed it was money he was owed. Small amounts at first and only a couple of payments here and there. Then the sums were getting bigger and from several different people, and he would say you keep this much for yourself and if you need any money you take it, just keep the rest safe for me. I am a highly intelligent person, and I knew deep down something wasn't right. However, I was also stupidly a very giving person remember, and I kept pushing down my suspicions and my discomfort because I wanted to help, I thought I was helping. I will also be very bluntly honest too, I was a single mum with three sons, and the extra money he was giving me was a significant factor, it was helping me, so that helped to turn down the volume on my discomfort.

Whenever I would get a little too uncomfortable and voice my concerns, he would always tell me how much he needed me, how he couldn't be without me. I was the only person he had, I was the only person he trusted and reel me back in again. People were now contacting me directly, girlfriends of other inmates and friends of other inmates. My suspicions became too loud, I couldn't quiet them down, and I couldn't ignore them anymore. I wasn't from that world, so I didn't know for sure what was happening, but I was smart enough to know it wasn't legal and it really wasn't right.

My smarts were finally taking over my giving without boundaries. And I began refusing to let different people put money in my account, now I was worried I didn't know what I was involved in, but I knew it wasn't right. He wasn't happy, and his approach now became pushier, I refused still. Now he wasn't all nicey-nicey, no more oh I need you, you're the only person I have and trust. No, now it was you better do this, I need that money, you are the one that I want to do this because I know you won't screw me over. Now nothing was keeping the volume low on my suspicions, and my discomfort was at an all-time high. I was afraid, I was terrified of what I had got myself into, and no amount of money could convince me to stay involved. I now refused point-blank to accept any payment from anyone, and I also refused to go see him again or buy him anything he needed. Then came the threats, nothing direct enough from him of course, he would say you will see what happens if you don't help me. Indirect threats that I knew were a threat, but it would be difficult to prove. I reported it to the prison and stopped all communication, the prison blocked him from calling me or writing to me directly. I kept £600 of his money after I did that, I don't know what I thought I was doing, but I indeed wasn't being smart. I think at the time I just thought I was getting out and washing my hands of the whole situation. Then came the calls from other people, and texts saying stuff like I know where you live and where your kids go to school, other things I can't remember now, there were lots. I reported it to the police, they took a statement and copies of the texts, just as I knew nothing was a direct enough threat to take any action. The police alerted the prison, and the prison moved him across the country. The threats didn't stop there though, and the police couldn't do anything, they said that unless there were explicit provable threats or if something happened in person they couldn't do anything.

I was so terrified by this point that I moved away, I moved without telling anyone where I was going. No forwarding address, not even my family. I packed everything in a van, and I just went taking two of my sons with me, my youngest son was living with his grandparents at that time, so I had to leave him behind. I changed my phone number, and also my name, that's how terrified I was and the lengths I went to, to get away. The threats stopped, and life slowly got back to normal, but just when I thought I had put it all behind me, the threats suddenly started again. I didn't know how, or who and I still couldn't prove a thing. They knew where I lived, and I was now in fear for my life and for my son's lives quite literally. I tried giving the money back, and they weren't interested in that, they said that wasn't enough it didn't make up for all the money lost, that they felt I was responsible for. They wanted me to get involved in getting money for them. I didn't even know what they wanted me to do, but I refused, and I kept refusing. The tipping point came when I got a message telling me this unknown person knew where my youngest son lived, and if I wanted to see him again, I had to sort this out. The penny dropped, I was travelling back up North every two weeks to see my son, and that's how they must have found me. At this point, I didn't feel the police could protect me, I had tried that several times. I really felt I had no other option but to sort this out, so I agreed to meet this person to get the details of what they wanted me to do. I know what you're thinking, what the fuck is she doing, believe me, if I were reading this I would be screaming it at the page. Terrified, I went to the place, I met with a sweet young guy, not what I was expecting at all, and I certainly wasn't what he was expecting. He gave me an envelope with a passport inside and some bank details, I was told that a loan had been approved in this woman's name and I was to sign the passport in that signature and go to a specific branch and collect £6000, and I was to bring it back to him. There is a reason I said this person was a sweet young guy, and in some ways, I need to thank him, because he really saved me from all of this nightmare. I'll explain, I asked him if I do this will it be over. He looked at me, and he said I should not tell you this, but you are so nice, and you really shouldn't be involved in this, you will not get out of this unless you get caught. I didn't quite understand, I said so they are going to want me to do more, and he said they will keep making you do this until you get caught, once you get caught you won't be any use to them anymore. The best thing you can do is get caught. It's a head fuck to be in that position, I didn't want to do it at all, and I certainly didn't want to get caught, but I couldn't see any other way out. I know you think I should have just gone to the police with the evidence in the envelope and believe me, I thought about it. The sweet guy cautioned me and told me that wouldn't end well for me either. So I went for it, I made the only decision I felt I could make at the time to end this nightmare. I went to the bank, I went inside knowing I was going to get caught. I didn't even sign the passport. I walked up to the window, I gave the teller the passport and told him I wanted to withdraw £6000 loan that had been deposited to that account, he looked at the passport, then looked at me for what felt like forever, he said give me a moment while I go arrange the withdrawal. He was gone for a few minutes, and I didn't know what was going on, I was praying, on the one hand, he didn't come back with £6000, and on the other hand, I was praying I didn't get caught. Between a rock and a hard place,

I believe that's referred to as. Have you ever been in a similar situation where you felt you were damned if you did and damned if you didn't? He came back and made an excuse about it taking a while longer than expected to get the cash and offered for me to sit upstairs for a few minutes while they tried to get it done. I followed him upstairs, and he took me into this very plush area reserved for business clients, he got me some water and left me to wait. Wait, this wasn't happening the way I imagined it was going to happen, I thought the police would have stormed the bank by now grabbed me and dragged me out in front of everyone. I was so nervous, my head was spinning it felt like I was going to have a heart attack, I started to think they were actually getting the money. I suddenly felt calm, I suddenly felt that they weren't getting the money, and it was going to be ok. It had dawned on me the police were coming, and it was really over. Just at that moment, I heard footsteps coming up the stairs, more than one person's footsteps coming up the stairs and there was the police, they spoke to me calmly, and they asked me just to follow them outside, they didn't want customers to really pay attention or be alarmed. They wanted me to just walk with them like nothing was wrong. I did, I was so calm, I smiled and just went with them. They took me outside and put me in a police van.

As we were driving away I was looking out of the back window for the sweet guy because I knew he was outside somewhere waiting for me and I saw him on the corner, he just tipped his head as if to say good for you. I felt that I had actually done the right thing. Finally, I felt inside I had made the right decision, I also felt I had stood up for myself (you know that part is always important to me) I took back Self, I took back my power, and I let Self be my weapon.

I told the police everything, they charged me with fraud. I had to go to court to prove my case, and I had all of the evidence I needed to prove my case. The evidence from the police, the prison, the texts and the letters. The judge took all of it into consideration and even commented on how he felt I had been let down by the system, he gave me a 12 month suspended sentence. Thankfully it was now actually over. Or perhaps not?

There's a lesson in this for all of us, believe me, I never thought I would have this story to tell, and I certainly didn't set out to create it. I am not going to justify one tiny bit of my actions in this situation, and I accept full responsibility for my part in it. However, I do want you to understand that it is so easy for any of us to find ourselves in a situation we feel like we can't control. I want you to see how easy it is for someone to manipulate us and it has nothing to do with intelligence, even the most highly intelligent people can be manipulated because the person doing the manipulating is parasitic they attach themselves to us, and they prey on our weaknesses, they prey on our vulnerabilities, and they use them to their advantage. They find us because we are givers with victim mentalities and we are the perfect victims for narcissistic people, they need us to feed off of, they need us just to make them feel better about themselves.

Master yourself, defy your Self inflicted suffering. We self impose suffering when we assume we are not enough. Believe the universe would not have wanted you born if you weren't made for something great. Don't let anybody be the puppet master of your life, cut the fucking strings, take back your power, take back Self. Let Self be your weapon. Smile and rise, smile and rise.

I don't know you yet, but I love you still.

# CHAPTER 11

## GOING TO PRISON

Yes I know, I fought, and I won the fraud case, however, what happed almost one year later. I had been on a driving ban due to all of the stress from before. The ban was now over, I had neglected to do was get my licence renewed after the ban. One day driving along I get pulled over by the police, I had my son Michael in the car and as we were pulling over I turned to Michael and I said I'm going to prison and he said what are you talking about I said I don't know I just know I'm in serious trouble, I just feel it. Trust me don't ask me to explain it I can't, but I just knew.

It was now 2009, just days away from the suspended sentence being over for the fraud. With a charge for driving while on a driving ban, and the added driving without insurance. I find myself going back to court, and I was under no illusion this was not going to go well, plus my lawyer had warned me it would most likely be a custodial sentence, I was prepared. I made arrangements for my sons, I left bank cards and credit cards at home and all the details with my son Michael for my accounts.

The judge took exception to this mistake, which was now one of many. There was no sympathy for what I had previously gone through, and I wasn't looking for any either. He sentenced me to ten weeks in prison, with good behaviour, I would serve five weeks. I was in shock, no matter how much I was prepared or expecting it, really I wasn't, there was always hope that under the circumstances the universe would conspire in my favour me again.

I didn't stop crying from the moment he gave his verdict, I cried the whole time I was in the holding cells downstairs, I cried when they put me on the bus, and I cried the entire time they were processing my arrival. I cried so much they were worried I was going to hurt myself. I must have cried for almost five days on and off, I was on what they call the induction wing, which is meant for new prisoners until they place you on a proper wing. That was the only wing where you could be in a cell on your own. I only came out of the cell to get my food and went straight back in, I didn't talk to anyone, I didn't want to know anyone, and I didn't want them knowing me either. The person in charge of the induction wing was so lovely and very helpful, he kept stalling my move to a proper wing and kept me on the induction until he could find a cell somewhere he felt I would cope. Finally, time ran out, and he couldn't stall anymore, he had to move me, I believe I was on there for almost three weeks, the maximum was meant to be seven days. However, during my time there, I was able to really spend time thinking about things and after the first five days of allowing myself to wallow and feel sorry for myself. I decided this wasn't going to beat me, I decided my mum hadn't put me on this earth to waste one-day let alone five weeks I took Self back again. So I did the only thing I could at that time, I got every self-help book from the library and read them over and over. Every chance I got, I went to the library to exchange books, there wasn't a lot of choices, but I learned everything anyway. I took notes and scribbled away like crazy, I started to make a plan for my life. I began to really focus on what I wanted from life and who I wanted to be, I began to think of the difference I could make in the world. I became absolutely determined that I wouldn't waste another day when I left there.

When I was moved onto a standard wing, I was moved onto a quiet side that had mostly enhanced non-violent people. I shared a cell with a woman that I became great friends with, I call her Z, she was there because she didn't have a visa for the UK and I helped her with her appeal, filling in all of the paperwork she had to complete and reading all of the paperwork they sent her. English wasn't her first language, and she was really struggling with everything. She also had terrible diabetes, and she wasn't coping very well. They put us together because they felt I would look after her, and she would be an excellent quiet person for me to be with. They were right. We inspired each other, we kept each other positive, and we shared a beautiful friendship. I learned what she had gone through in her own country, the terrible, unbelievable acts of violence, sexual abuse and the death of some of her family members. She managed against all the dds s to make it to the UK with her husband, and her son was born in the UK. I knew her story to be true because of the pain in her eyes when she entrusted me to hear her and believe her, and I also read it in her paperwork. I understand now that I was there for her, I think that this is where I really began stepping into myself and who I was meant to be, how I wanted to show up in this world and the work I have become so passionate about now. She inspired me, her struggle and her pain made me want to help as many people as possible. It's part of the reason I support women and girls and why I plan to launch my own foundation. I have always been passionate about the crisis that other women like Z face, my mum always brought me up with some awareness. However, this was the first time in my life, I was not only facing a real survivor of such atrocities. I was sharing a room, food, a toilet and my life with her and she was sharing hers with me. We ate, slept and shit together, and I could not be more proud to have shared that with her and to call her my friend. I came face to face with who I wanted to be. I met her son and her husband, we wrote to each other. I went back to visit her, being a fellow inmate, I had to wait two months before I was allowed to see her. We kept in touch, and I saw her after she went home, she says it's because of me that she got to go back to her son and her husband. No it's because of her, she had so much determination and will to get to the UK, to begin to have her life and her family, and she never gave up on getting back to her family, she already had everything she needed inside her. The universe just brought me to support her and provide a little backup (I'm an excellent backup, even if I do say so myself, giggle).

Due to a delay and a mistake with my paperwork being processed by probation I could not be released at five weeks, they gave me a choice I could be released a week late with an ankle bracelet for another 4 weeks which would have taken me to the full ten weeks sentence or I could choose to stay a further 3 weeks and go home free. I could of course complain and appeal to get the paperwork corrected, but that wouldn't have done much good, because I would be gone by the time it ever got processed, let alone fixed. So I did what I can't believe still today, I opted to stay, and I ended up serving eight weeks, and two days in total, I came home August 10th 2009, August 10th was a very significant day for me, not just because I was going back, but because it would have been my mums birthday and I saw this as a sign. I guess I really was meant to be there after all (smile).

I won't go into all of the details of the time I spent in there, because it's just not relevant. Let's just say it wasn't easy, I was attacked and hit in the face, I had hot coffee thrown on me, and some people tried to intimidate me verbally, the funny thing is the more they did these things to me the more I stepped into myself. They didn't like that I didn't shy away and get scared, but I also didn't retaliate. They didn't know how to deal with me. I certainly wasn't meant to be there, and that's not what I say that's what some of the other inmates told me, for various reasons. Some didn't like me because I wasn't meant to be there, they didn't like my presence because I wasn't like them. One inmate that really didn't like me (although I suspect secretly she did and I would even go as far as saying she respected and admired me) told me that she felt my presence on the wing when I wasn't near her. She could hear my voice, and she could see how I carried myself, and she didn't like it. She said that I walked around as though I was better than them. She would go out of her way to speak to me and attempt to goad me, but these little battles of the mind always resulted in her getting angry and at herself mainly. We all know that I was a source for her insecurities to come flooding out and since everyone else was scared of her she gravitated to me like a moth to a flame for stimulation mainly I suspect. Some said I wasn't meant to be there because they liked me, and they also felt I had a presence that was positive, kind and loving, and that I wasn't meant for there. I want to tell you now, however, horrible the difficulties were, and there was a lot not mentioned. I choose to focus on the positive and the good that came out of that time. I quickly became the go-to person for advice, encouragement and care and I'm grateful for that, I'm thankful for the experiences in that building with the people I met that have helped shape who I am today.

I can honestly say the whole experience contributes to who I am and how I choose to show up in the world now, it's really the first time in my life I began to realise just how powerful my presence was, how I could inspire, advise, empower, encourage and bring positivity to those who need it and challenge those who don't think they need it. I learned a lot about myself that's for sure, I also discovered my limits were few and my strength infinite. I learned the universe is always conspiring in your favour and life happens for you, not to you. You just have to choose what you do with what life throws at you, that's the critical part.

I joke, and I say I had an eight-week break to focus on myself and take time to see who I could become at Her Majesties pleasure and it was for free.

Nothing is ever free (it's just my sense of humour and how I choose to deal with things). I lost time with my sons because I was in prison, I lost my business because I was in jail. I lost my home because I was in prison. I had to fight to rebuild my life when I got home. I was so ready to fight the world when I came out of there, I had this absolute determination that those eight weeks were going to mean something. I was going to achieve everything I ever wanted, and I realised some pretty wild dreams. I also learned if you want everything in your wildest imagination, your imagination has to be pretty damn wild in the first place. I fought in court and got my equipment and furniture back from my business. I found an investor for my business one month after coming home, I found new premises, and I began to rebuild. I fought the people who thought they could destroy me with a story in the newspaper, so I gave the full story myself instead. I challenged those who called the centre manager where my business was now located because I told him everything in person. I lost so much in those eight weeks, and I had to fight the consequences for a long time after, but what I gained in the process can never be taken away.

I learned how to be me, I learned how to use my presence powerfully, I learned that being bold meant being vulnerable, and it also meant being fearless. Be all of you, through suffering, but recognising. You have to recognise what you've gone through without being a victim to it. You must be the owner of your suffering, you must accept both the light and the dark, without the dark, there is no light. And that actually gave me pride. I realised that very few people could turn around what I did. I was able to turn around every single negative thing in my life, everything, use it for power and use it for fuel. I realised I would always be ok if I just kept moving forward.

I knew deep down that my foundation was broken, I had to rebuild. I had to pick up this broken-ass house that was me, pick myself up, get all this fucking concrete, I had to lay this fucking land beautiful and flat, get all the shit out, rebuild this foundation and put this fucking house back on an excellent foundation. That foundation now is This Woman Michelle Margaret Marques (MMM). I had to recreate myself to This Woman (the woman that I wanted to be) not what the world made me, not what life made me. Life experience made me a scared, angry, insecure, needy girl. When you are a woman, and you look at that mirror every fucking day of your life, and you do not like the reflection staring back at you, if you choose to live in that, that is your fault. We have the ability to recreate ourselves, and I decided to recreate myself in the form of This Woman. That is a person that said, I'm not going to be this, this woman that's insecure, afraid and broken. I want to be This Woman. I want to be my own hero. I want to be a woman that I look up to. I want to see me and be proud of me. I want to look in that reflection and be proud of the representation looking back at me. But the only way I'm going to do that is to take out that big suitcase of shit that I was in my life. I had to start emptying it. And Michelle Moffat couldn't do that. That's much too frightening, This Woman (MMM) had to go back there and say, I got this shit. Let's go. Let's woman the fuck up. So that's where This Woman comes from. It's a person I had to create to start handling how to fix Michelle Moffat.

I've realised in life that you have to take Self back every day, it's not a case of taking her back once, and now you're fixed, or you're triumphant, no you have to take her back every single day until no one can ever take her from you again. Until you have mastered yourself, this whole entire journey we are all on is about mastering ourselves. The universe is always conspiring in our favour, and I believe the universe was most definitely conspiring in my favour that day. When else or how else was I going to give myself eight weeks to work on myself, to step away from my life, my sons and my business for eight weeks to fully and totally focus on my life? It wasn't going to happen, not at that time, not without the knowledge I now have, and the journey of personal development life has taken me on from that day forward.

Recreate yourself, woman the fuck up. Take Self back. You know you can. (smile)

I don't know you yet, but I love you still.

# CHAPTER 12

## MY BROTHER SLOWLY KILLED HIMSELF

My brother was my best friend growing up, we were always together. We were always having fun and doing silly things, we went everywhere together. I was a proper tomboy, always covered in mud and hanging around with all of my brother's friends. (you wouldn't think it now huh, smile)

After my mum passed away, my brother was never the same person, he began taking drugs and getting in trouble. He had gotten himself into a bit of trouble before this. But nothing like he was doing now and not with the people he was now spending his time with. My mum died two days before my brother's 18th birthday, it was tough. We never really talked about her as a family, my father hit the bottle hard after my mum died, and we just didn't have any proper grieving.

My brother went down a path that he just couldn't control and no matter how hard I tried, he just didn't come back fully. There were times when he would do well, and it would seem like he finally found his way back, finally found the turning point, but the wind would change, and he would be lost again. It took him years of destroying himself, years of pain and suffering. Years of addiction and going in and out of prison. Years of doing bad things to people he loved and I was no exception, he did many things to me over the years that included stealing from my home, assaulting me and emptying my entire bank account, but I loved him still.

The last time I ever saw my brother alive was when he badly assaulted me, he had been staying with me because I was the only one who would actually take him in. I'm not going to get into all of the details, I just want to give you some context to the story. This time was different though this time I warned him that if he took anything from me again I was disowning him and I would press charges. I watched him go through drug withdrawal on my sofa, and this was not the first time. Three days of watching him rolling around in excruciating pain telling me he was going to die, sweating and breathing heavy. Crying and screaming in pain, begging me to get him some drugs. It finally passed, and he was slowly getting better. A few weeks passed by, and he was starting to gain weight and look healthy, he seemed happier and was beginning to talk about his future, and I really began to hope that this was it, this was finally the turning point. I finally had my little brother back. I came home early one day, and he wasn't there, immediately I just knew, not my first time here either. I ran upstairs opened my wardrobe pulled all of the things out to get to my jewellery box which I had hidden, and everything was gone apart from my mum's ring and necklace (how kind huh) I called my father and told him. I also told him that's it I'm done I warned him this was the last time he would do this to me, (it wasn't about the things it was the hurt and the betrayal). The pain of watching him fight this battle over and over again, I couldn't do it anymore, and I wasn't going to allow him to put me through it anymore. I couldn't put my sons through it anymore. I called the police and reported him, I told my father to come to get his things, don't bring him here and don't allow him to come here, the police are looking for him, and if he comes here I will call them. Later that night my father, his wife and my brother came to my house, I was cooking dinner, and they just let themselves in.

Michael was watching tv in the front room, Stephen was out somewhere (thank god, because he would have gotten involved) and Liam was at his grandparents.

I told them to get out, I had made myself clear earlier. I did not want him there, and I was going to call the police. An argument ensued, and I began to call the police I walked away into the hallway, I locked the front door and put the key in my pocket.

At this point, all three of them were screaming at me and trying to stop me from calling the police, all three of them at some point in this situation assaulted me (yes you heard that correctly) I did say all three of them. It lasted about 15 minutes, screaming and shouting and fending off blows and trying to defend myself. Then at some point, there was a break in the noise, and we could hear Michael screaming in the front room terrified, I said that's your grandson in there screaming while you all beat his mother up, this made them stop. My brother ran upstairs and climbed out of an upstairs window dropped down onto the roof of my car, smashed the back windscreen of my car with my son's hockey stick and ran off.

When I came back downstairs, my father and his wife were sat in my front room as if nothing had happened and they were there for a visit. The police arrived and arrested them both, they gave her a caution because she had admitted hitting me and she didn't have a criminal record. They charged my father with grievous bodily harm. My brother was eventually caught, after making lots of threats against me to drop the charges, so he was charged with grievous bodily harm, criminal damage, intimidating a witness and threating criminal damage. My father and my brother both plead not guilty at the pre-trial hearing. People in my family and friends could not believe that I had my father and brother charged and went ahead with a court trial, I was raising three sons, and it was my responsibility to teach them they could not behave like that and no one, not even their own family was allowed to treat them like that. My brother didn't turn up to court and while I was waiting in the witness room waiting for the trial to begin against my father the court clerk came and he told me the trial had been cancelled as my father had now changed his plea to guilty and they didn't need me as a witness. My father received a 12 month suspended sentence. My brother went on the run and was never caught. I never saw him again, and I never spoke to him again. He would call whenever I was at my sister's and beg to talk to me, but I never spoke to him.

Nine years passed by, and I refused to speak to him each time. In that time, he had continued his addiction to drugs and alcohol. And was now married to a woman who also had a problem with alcohol. I was at home one night in January 2011. I was pregnant with my daughter at that time. It was late, after 10 pm and my phone rang, it was my sister, and I was annoyed that she was calling me so late. She told me my brother was in the hospital in Glasgow and he's dying, my sister was always very dramatic, so I told her to stop being so emotional and explain. She said the nurse had told them he only had 24 hours or less to live. I just thought this was crazy, I thought she was just over the top. I spoke with my uncle who had now arrived at the hospital, and he told me, he's in a critical way Michelle a real bad way. If you want to see him before he goes, you better get here tonight. I was living at least five hours away from Glasgow at that time, we left immediately and went to pick my sister up on the way, she lived over 2 hours away from me.

Anyway, on our way driving as fast as we could it was now, 4 am, or so we are 30 minutes away from Glasgow and my phone rings. It was my uncle, when I answered I said we're 30 minutes away we are almost there, he said he's gone, he's just gone Michelle, you're too late. We got to the hospital, and I just couldn't go in the room. I didn't know how I was feeling, so much had happened. I stood in the doorway, but I just couldn't go in. As we were leaving the hospital, I had the urge to go back alone to see him. I entered the room this time, but I just couldn't go near him, he didn't look like him, he didn't look like my brother. I stood by the bottom of the bed, and I said to him, you stupid, stupid boy, you had a whole life ahead of you, you wasted a perfectly good life, 36 years of life, wasted and you could have done so much in this world. I was busy giving him a right telling off, if you get the chance to come back, if there is such a thing as an afterlife, you better do amazing things, you better make a difference in this world, you better make it right. When a nurse walked in, she said it's ok you can go up to him, you can touch him, I said no I don't know who that is he doesn't even look like my brother, and she said he must have been a handsome boy in his time and I said yes he looked like me, we laughed, (we were the spitting image of each other growing up). He was 36 years of age, and he died of liver sorosis, can you imagine how much abuse he must have done to himself what he must have put himself through to kill himself like that. I picked his things up from the morgue, I picked up his death certificate, and I went to see his wife who I had never met before. She couldn't even understand what we were trying to tell her, bedridden and not very with us mentally, he was her carer apparently. The place they lived was run down, and the house was disgusting, my feet were sticking to the floor. When we left the house I said to my uncle he's better off where he is now, it's better than that (of course I never would have wanted him dead, but after seeing how his life was, I knew he was in a better place, he was with his mum). His wife died exactly two weeks later of the same disease. My uncle and I planed his funeral and made all the arrangements.

I believe my brother never really got over my mum's death. I believe he was lost, and he could just never find his way back. He wasn't an evil person, he wasn't a thug like everyone thought, the person lying in that coffin wasn't my brother, he wasn't the brother I knew, the brother I grew up with. My brother was a beautiful, kind, loving, warm, generous and fun person who was always full of life and smiling and would have done anything to help anyone. He was just broken, and he didn't know how to fix himself. These are the things I actually what I wrote in his eulogy, I was the only person that spoke at his funeral. I also talked about the kind of person he was, the friendship we had, the things I loved about him, and how I had actually lost him a long time ago. Everyone cried, they said it was beautiful, and they couldn't believe I wrote it, the person he had arguably hurt the most, the person who charged him with assault, the person who had turned her back on him. It took a lot for me to write that eulogy and it took a lot to focus on the positives about my brother, to focus on the friendship we had once shared and the things I loved about him. I spent a long time wishing I had got there before he died, if I had only gotten there in time I could have told him I loved him, I could have been there for him at the end, that's been the hardest thing for me, even now. Despite wrestling with a lot of emotions, regrets and guilt I managed to find the good and the love, and I also managed to find peace in the fact I had done everything I ever could for him, and I never turned my back on him, I always had love for him, I still had hope for him and I always wanted the best for him and he always knew it.

I may not have made it there in time, I may not have been in his life for the last nine years, but I was there in the way I was meant to be and in the end, I was always there when it mattered the most. I just had to protect my family and live my life, my way with my choices.

Make the choices that serve your life, don't let anyone change or influence what you need to do for you or your family no matter what. I took a lot of criticism for the choices I made after those events. I did what I had to do for my life, that didn't mean I stopped loving him or I stopped wanting the best for him, it also didn't mean that I ever stopped hoping for a better outcome. I always imagined one day he would finally clean his act up, and we would be best friends again. I just never imagined that I would have to find that friendship still in my heart instead of real life. He made his choices, and I made my choices. You make your choices.

I don't know you yet, but I love you still.

# CHAPTER 13

## MY MARRIAGE BREAKDOWN

I left my daughter's dad, (in fact I was the one that had left all of my relationships) I was absolute in my determination to not stay in an unhappy relationship that I manifested it every time. This is going to be a short one, the story here is not really in the relationship although I could tell you that I wasn't happy, there was no love, and the relationship was not great, that's obvious. We (I) tried to fix it for a long time, longer than I should have and just couldn't.

I want the story and the lesson here to reflect the worth we should have for ourselves and the courage we should and need to summon sometimes to move forward with going after what we want and deserve in our life's. It's not about blame, who was wrong or right, it's not about the bad but rather the good. The good in the sense that we had a relationship and we were in love once, we have a beautiful amazing daughter, we got married in a beautiful church in Barbados, we had a beautiful reception with a small group of people we love, and we always gave the best of ourselves to our daughter.

I walked away because I wanted more, more from a relationship and more from life. I wanted my daughter to have more and to know that she came from a loving relationship. I wanted her to know what a loving relationship was. To understand how to be in a loving relationship. I wanted her to know she was absolutely loveable and worth nothing less than the most amazing loving relationship.

I've never had the kind of relationship I have always truly wanted, but I won't ever settle for less. Being madly in love, excited to be with each other, proud of each other, a great connection and a deep bond. Enjoying the heck out of life with each other and building an amazing, loving relationship together. I want to have a deep connection and a real partnership in every way with my person. Build a life and a relationship with my best friend. Something beyond ordinary, built on trust and friendship, building a dream. Support each other, push each other to achieve more. Love deeply and cherish each other. The kind of relationship that makes the world jealous when they see us together. And I want my daughter to grow up in that kind of relationship, to model her relationship on that kind of relationship. What a beautiful gift you want to give your daughter some people have said. Of course, it is a wonderful gift. However, it's the kind of beautiful gift we should all give ourselves and our children. That is the kind of relationship we should all have for ourselves and the standard we should have for our life's. Some have said my standard is too high, some have said I want too much, it isn't realistic or obtainable. I say that's bullshit, absolute and total bullshit. You are the creator of your life, and you are the only person who gets to choose what you want and set your standards. Don't ever settle, passionately protest mediocrity. You deserve what You want, set Your standards set them fucking high. If they aren't high, you can't fly.

I'm not suggesting you go off and leave your partner because it isn't exciting or that you should go off chasing some fairytale, no. I am saying you should have the kind of relationship you want and if you aren't currently getting that then you have to, first get clear on what you do want, then change what you have by either working at it to get what you want and if you can change it, get the fuck out and go after what you do want, have the courage to give yourself the beautiful gift of everything you have ever dreamed of in your life and your relationship. You won't regret it.

My daughter's dad isn't a horrible person, he's just not my person. He didn't want to put the work in, he didn't want to fly high, he was happy enough with the way it was, and I just wasn't.

I had to fly, I had to have something vibrating higher. I have to have my person, I have to have my standard. Set your standards high and don't ever let anyone convince you they are too high. Have the courage and the conviction to go after what you truly want, don't ever settle.

Fly, fly, fly.

I don't know you yet, but I love you still.

# CHAPTER 14

## JOURNEY TO THE NEW ME

The journey to the new me began in 2009 when I was in prison. That changed me as a person, not just because I was in there and my freedom had been taken away. The change happened when I began to focus on myself and really work on myself. It also had a lot to do with the experience I had in there and the people I met, particularly Z. I was always interested in personal development before, I had read books and gone to seminars. However, now, I couldn't get enough. I wanted to learn everything I could, and I seriously wanted to work on myself. My mind was so open to everything, and I was really enjoying learning. It's a journey I will always be on, I do at least one hour of personal development every day. That may be listening to an audiobook, a meditation, visualisation, or working on a transformational course such as Life Book. These are just some examples, it just really depends on what my goal or focus is at any given time.

Although the journey developed there, it took on a whole different direction after I came home. I was hell-bent on changing everything, I knew I was going to have to fight to rebuild my life. I decided I was going to face everything head-on, and I was finally going to step into me fully. I began such a personal journey, and I set out on an entire discovery of myself. Every course on healing, I could get my hands on or attend. Healing grief, healing anger, healing abuse, healing love, healing your inner child, I could go on and on. Let's just say if it had healing in the title I most likely did it. (smile) Then a whole bunch of courses and seminars on stepping into your true potential. Things like Tony Robins Unleash the power within, Success summits, walked on fire, (more than once). Many Mindvalley courses and quests, Lisa Nichols, Marisa Peer. The list is endless, anything in the personal development world that relates to creating the life you want. Or transforming yourself I done it, including twelve-hour chanting sessions and horse meditation. You get the picture I think, I'm obsessed with personal development (giggle).

The journey itself takes its biggest twist after my daughter was born. I feel I not only gave birth to her, but I gave birth to a new me. I think this is where I really began to be the real me, me I always wanted to be, me I knew deep down I still was. She had just gotten lost somewhere under all of the stress, anger and grief. I felt complete now, I felt life had given me a second chance, a chance to get it right now. I knew I was going to be the mother I had always so desperately tried to be, but I was going to do it so differently. I had learned from my wounds. I was going to teach her to be the woman I always wanted to be and then some. I was going to give her so much love, she would never have to question what love was. That is one thing I knew I could do, despite the mistakes I made with my boys I always gave love.

I had a complicated pregnancy from the beginning with my daughter, and my pelvis actually collapsed too. I was in constant and sometimes excruciating pain. I couldn't walk properly, couldn't sit or get up from a chair on my own, and I also couldn't go to the bathroom on my own. It took almost one year after she was born for me to begin to really take control of the situation and set back up my business again. I had around ten months of physiotherapy, to help recover, and I was told not to go back to running my salon and being a massage therapist. I wasn't about to accept that, I said to the physiotherapist in no uncertain terms. I fully intended to set my business back up, I couldn't imagine a world where I didn't see my clients and do massage, and she could either help me to deal with it or not. The first three vertebrae of my spine, where being crushed due to the angle of my pelvis, and standing doing massage all day was not going to make that better. She taught me some stretches that I could use throughout the day and stand in a half squat all the time. For six months, I was in pain twenty-four/seven, I started my day doubled over and ended it the same way. Eventually, the pain got less, and some days were good, and only some were bad. I was determined not only to rebuild my business again but to be an active woman and mum still.

Before my pregnancy, I used to work out hard. I had a personal trainer three times per week, I went to the gym four-five times a week, and I went for a run around the lake most lunchtimes. That had become my way of dealing with stress. I had also lost a lot of weight around eighty-four lbs. After my pregnancy and my recovery from my pelvis collapsing, I had now gained one hundred and thirty-three lbs. This was my next path on the journey to the new me. My weight loss journey wasn't just a weight loss journey, it really became my journey to the inner me and another part of the real me. I had let go of a lot of emotional baggage I had carried and so much of what had been holding me back. I just had one final road to navigate, and that was to reveal all of me underneath by shedding the emotional padding and protection I had been carrying through various parts of my adulthood. I had weight challenges throughout my entire adulthood, like so many of us. I would lose weight, and I would gain more back, up and down and up and down. This time was no exception, except it was. This time I had done the work, this time, I knew what the problem was, and this time I could fix it with the right solution. Of course, it was due to my pelvis issue that I couldn't walk properly, let alone exercise. But I was also doing what I had always done eating my pain and my emotion. This was physical and emotional pain this time and not feeling loved in my marriage, this required a lot more stuffing back down and therefore, a lot more eating. Before I left my husband, I already knew I had to process my emotions, and I needed to work on me more.

That's when my most in-depth journey of all started, I made the decision to take that road, not just to shed the weight, but to shed every single bit of my past and really take back Self. I learned to love myself and put myself first. I left my husband, I let go of one hundred and forty-nine lbs, my business was now thriving, and so was I. I actually now loved myself deeply enough. I launched my skincare brand, I became a sexual abuse coach. I found my purpose, I set up my brand and began my mission. No more eating pain or carrying around my past, no more emotional baggage, guilt and anger. I have learned to live in the present moment and focus so much more on pure joy and love every day. I am a desire seeker and an adventure lover. I am creating my life the way I have always wanted to, and I can tell you, you can only get there by doing the work you need to do on yourself. I say this many times in this book, take back Self. She is extraordinary when you set her free.

I don't know you, yet, but I love you still.

# CHAPTER 15

## CLAIMS OF SEXUAL ABUSE

January 2016 while on a visit to Paris and Versailles I received a call from my oldest son Stephen, it's a phone call I will probably never forget. He sounded flustered and concerned, he said I know you're away mum, but I had to call you. He told me that my sister had been to see him and had said some really awful things about me, I laughed and told him not to worry. Stephen said, but mum, you don't understand, the things she has said are horrible. I laughed again and said yes don't worry she's always saying terrible things about me. Stephen said no this time it's very different, and I don't know how to tell you. I said ok now you are worrying me, what has she said about me this time, he stuttered and stammered and couldn't get his words out. I was getting frustrated, and I said just tell me, he kept repeating I don't know how to. I said just say it, blurt it out it's ok I'm used to it by now. I was very used to being on the receiving end of nasty comments and defamations of my character from my sister. This was nothing new for me (or so I thought). However, my son had never sounded this worked up before. Finally, he blurted out Aunt Rose has accused you of sexually abusing her since she was little, and that you did it all her life.

Excuse me? I said, what did you just say. He said I know mum I don't know how else to tell you, I shouldn't have to say such a thing. She came to see me and spent about two hours telling me all of these details and then she asked me if you had ever sexually abused me if you had ever touched me anywhere. I told her no way, I don't know how you can ask such a thing.

He was right, this time it was very different, this time I wasn't laughing, this time I was in shock, I was angry, very fucking angry. Up to this point, I had been through a lot with my sister. She had her issues, and I had always supported and helped her. This was another level of hurt and defamation even for her. I couldn't stop thinking about this vile accusation. It was going over and over in my mind, I couldn't understand this. What was her motivation? Why was she saying these things about me? I had a long time to think about it before I could actually do anything about it before I could see her face to face and try to make sense of it. As I said I was travelling, in fact, I was on a coach trip, the only time I ever took a couch trip out of the country alone, so you can imagine I did nothing but think about it. I decided I was going to go there and see her when I got back in the country, I decided I wanted to see her face to face and hear her

MICHELLE MARGARET MARQUES

accusations and explanations for myself. I didn't live close to her, so it took a few days to make this possible.

Let me explain some things so that you get some perspective, I am five years older than my sister. How she was describing this accusation to my son sounded like she was around two years old when this alleged abuse began. She would say she's been doing this to me since I was yay big and put her hand out like the size of a toddler. I was seven years old when this alledged abuse began, and she claims this had happened all her life. She was basically describing me as a monster, in my opinion. A sexual predator, a vile disgusting and depraved human being. These are the kind of images and words of description that I think of when I think of the accusations she made against me, and I'm sure you do too. The pain was unbearable.

Let me also give you some further perspective, this girl lived with me, after my mum died I took her and my father to live with me. She also lived with me as an adult, of her own free will, in fact, she didn't just make a choice to live with me once in her adulthood, she lived under my roof during several separate periods. She even asked to be placed with me by probation when she was released from prison. I was present in her life throughout, I visited her regularly in prison. I sent her money, I took care of her through every low and every high. I was always her first call when she needed anything, especially money. I was there during labour when her firstborn, my niece was born, my niece would stay with me, and I would take her out on the weekends alone. In fact, I was present in all of her five children's life's until they were taken by social services, due to her personal issues, and I will not discuss this. I was part of all of the proceedings with social services and the court process, I travelled up and down the country every two weeks for meetings and court appearances. I am godmother to all five of her children. I always supported her, and I always tried my very best to be a positive, encouraging, loving force in her life. I gave her a job and wanted to teach her to want more from life (she told me she had lowered herself to work for me). And for reasons only she can explain, no matter how hard I tried she resented me more, the more I tried, the more she disliked me or hated me as it felt to me. I honestly couldn't have been there more for this girl than I was, I didn't treat her like my sister, I treated her like my child, she was 14 when my mum died she needed me. Anyway, let's get back to the story.

It was also my youngest son Liam's birthday, so I took him for lunch when I arrived in the area, to celebrate with him and relax a while before I confronted this situation. He came with me so that I would have a witness (little did I know how much

I was actually going to need a witness). I thought I was just being smart and protecting myself from any further accusations. However, no one could have predicted what was about to come and exactly why a witness was the most important thing I needed. The moment I knocked on her front door, she immediately began shouting through the window that she didn't want to talk to me and that if I didn't get away from her door, she was going to smash my face in and smash my car up. I told her that's fine, but I'm going nowhere until you explain. Why you are accusing me of sexually abusing you since you were little and apparently I've done this all of your life. She was going crazy at this point screaming oh you want the neighbours to hear, yes, in fact, I did want the neighbours to hear. I wanted everyone to hear, I had nothing to fear, nothing to hide. So yes I wanted the whole street to hear if that's what she wanted, I never shied away from anything in my life and I sure as hell wasn't going to shy away from this vile situation.

She came outside, screaming at the top of her lungs like a crazy person, that she was going to smash my face in and smash my car up if I didn't go away. I told her, please do. If you feel that is what you need to do. I am going to do what I need to do. I want to know why you are accusing me of sexually abusing you. Why now out of the blue at the age of 36. She began screaming; you did sexually abuse me since I was yay big. You touched me, and you made me touch you, and you have done it my whole life. I was asking her to explain the details and to explain why she didn't cut me out of her life the moment she was old enough? Why I was allowed anywhere near her kids let alone be their godmother?

She just kept repeating the same accusations and screaming that she was going to destroy my life, destroy my business. Saying you think you are so amazing with your life and your business. You think you're so smart, I'm going to destroy it all. The neighbours that were in their homes that day were now out in the street, because of the noise. My son and I had gone to the other side of the road at this point. She then begins shouting across the street to my son I'm so sorry you have to find out like this, you have to find out what kind of a person your mother is, my son told her she was a liar. And she started shouting at him. That was the point I had enough, my anger came raging out, not for me, not for the vile accusations against me, but for my son. I screamed, don't you dare say that to him, don't you dare apologise that he needs to find out like this. That he needs to find out what kind of person I am, you should be apologising for putting him through this at all. I told her she was disgusting, and she began to cross the road shouting that she was going to smash my face in. I began to cross the street towards her, she longed at me, pushing me to the ground. Forcibly projecting saliva into her mouth and spitting it in my face then shouting that's what I think of you.

I picked myself up and called the police, I reported that she had assaulted me and asked for them to attend immediately. My son and I continued to stand on the other side of the road while I waited for the police to arrive. While we were standing there, she was shouting telling the neighbours her accusations ane telling me that she had told My Sisters Place all about what I had done and they were going to prosecute me, they believed her and that my father knew all about it and believed her too. I didn't know what My Sisters Place was, but I later found out, it ironically was a women's refuge for abused women. One of the neighbours from the house I happened to be standing outside, said to me, my sister and I can be nasty to each other when we fight, but I've never done anything like this to her. We chatted and agreed it was awful. The police arrived, and one officer spoke to me while the other officer took her inside her house. I told the officer what had happened and agreed to go ahead with official action against her. However, I also asked him if he could arrest me so that he could investigate these accusations she was making. He said he couldn't just arrest me or take me for questioning. The officer said that he would have to take a statement from her. Investigate it, and if there were any case against me, then he would arrest me. I said ok do that then please, I so badly at that point wanted to prove myself innocent and stop this whole movie-like situation, that's what it felt like to me. He left me outside and went into her house, he came back a short while later and told me although she claimed the accusations were true and she had explained her allegations to him in detail, she was not prepared to make a formal complaint and refused to give a statement. The reason she gave, was because she's my sister, hmm yeah that didn't stop her from doing this to me I said. I asked him what I could do about it, and he said I couldn't really do anything unless she made a formal complaint.

I could not believe what he was saying, I pushed again, surely you can take my statement and conduct an investigation I will come with you now, he said without the victim (the victim I thought) making it official his hands were tied. I told him that she had also claimed that this My Sisters Place was going to take me to court and prosecute me. He said he couldn't see how that would be possible because any action would only be possible after an official complaint and an investigation that proved there was a case to answer. I said so she is just free to run around making accusations of this kind and there is nothing I can do to prove I'm innocent, to protect my reputation. She claims she intends to destroy me, my life and my business and I can't do anything about it. He said well you can take an injunction against her if she persists, or you could take a civil suit against her. He advised me to report any harassment or continued accusations to the police. Which I have had to do and she has received a warning for. There was nothing else he could do, and I was left feeling helpless.

The police officers arrested her for the assault and took her away in the police car. I was given instructions to attend the police station later that day with my son to provide statements, which we did. She was charged with assault and released later that day. I was really hoping that while she was in the police station being interviewed, she would make the accusations official. I was told when I made my statement, that she had claimed her accusations were valid during the interview but did not want to make it official.

Meanwhile, during a visit to my father's house that day, I discover she had told him the same accusations two weeks earlier, and he had just told her she was being stupid and asked why this didn't come out earlier, why she hadn't told him or anyone else. When I asked why he hadn't seen fit to inform me. He responded that he decided to just ignore it because he thought it would just blow over. Hmm, really I thought to myself, I told him he should have informed me despite how he felt about it. I said to him, apparently My Sisters Place is going to prosecute me, he replied yes she told me that too, and she also told me you believe her, he denied believing her. I contacted My Sisters Place and after some back and forth and a manager being consulted they agreed to discuss the situation with me, they initially claimed they could not talk with me about my sister because of data protection. I told her I don't need you to discuss one detail about my sister. However, I do need you to discuss my own situation, my personal assault and my own abuse because I am now a victim of this act, and I am being told you are prosecuting me. Therefore, I have a right to know if this is true, and by law, you have to discuss this situation with me. You are not being asked to disclose details about my sister, you are being asked to listen to my circumstances. We discussed the accusations and the situation from my point of view, and I was told that while my sister had discussed some details with them regarding me, that they were not in a position to prosecute me and they had advised police involvement which she refused.

I later found out that a friend of my sisters had been given a new house to live in, in a beautiful area by My Sisters Place and that they had also provided new furniture for the home. I have never confirmed this to be accurate as it's not relevant to my life. However, this information makes me believe (and these are solely my belief's, possibly the only way my brain can make sense of it) that my sister made up this whole story in an attempt to also be moved by My Sisters Place and receive everything that her friend had been given. I was told that she never received any assistance from My Sisters Place due to the fact she did not move forward with an official complaint against me. I believe that she took these lies so far that she now couldn't get out of it and had to see it through. What I don't understand is why she continues to maintain these lies years later and has continued to cause friction in my family with my sons, with her children and in my life with accusations she refuses to back up, as I said earlier I was forced to report her to the police a second time for continuing to make these accusations.

They told me if she continued to make the accusations without reporting it officially they would arrest her for harassment. And advised me to continue to report any incidents as they would then be able to take action against her. She was given a warning. She maintains her accusations are correct, but has still failed to take official action. I have never allowed her in my life since that day in January 2016, and I never will. However, I have been told that she comments on my success and how proud she is, how proud that I'm her sister and that she thinks I'm going to have my own TV show like Oprah one day (which I am, of course, smile)

I don't understand how anyone could even speak the person's name that had done the vile things she accused me of, let alone boast and brag about how proud they are of them. Truth is no matter how much I have worked in this inside and no matter how much I have unpicked it and put it back together, it will never make sense, it is just something I accept as part of my story now, I have to just adjust to it. It may never make sense to me that anyone let alone my family member could make false accusations of any kind let alone the magnitude of these accusations. However, I will also not run away and hide from it. As an actual victim of sexual abuse, these accusations have hurt me so very deeply. However, more importantly, she has made a mockery of pain and suffering that actual victims of sexual abuse go through when they report these incidents and the courage they have to summon to get through the legal process of proving themselves and having people believe them. She's making it easier for people to ignore women when they do have the courage to come forward.

In my opinion and in my experience, victims of sexual abuse don't usually by choice stay around the person who has or is abusing them, they don't allow that abuser to be around their kids, they don't often go around suddenly after 30+ years visiting family members for a cup of tea and blurting it out, they don't usually go to a women's refuge unless they are very ready to face it or they need to get away from it, they don't often go running around the streets shouting about it to all the neighbours, they don't usually tell their children about it unless they have to, they most certainly don't often say it to their nephews and they absolutely don't usually wait for the abuser to call the police and then inform the police it's accurate several different times but then refuse to make an official statement. They don't usually brag and broadcast how proud they are of the fruitful life the abuser has. I certainly wouldn't, and I've never worked with a sexual abuse victim who has taken this course of action (non-action)

I want to give you some facts about what actual victims of sexual abuse go through, as well as being one, I work with a lot of them.

One in four women will be abused in our lifetime, 90% of those women don't report it. Half of them, suffer in silence never telling anyone, because it involves a family member or someone they know, the other half through fear of not being believed. They are right because we don't believe them, we don't believe women of sexual abuse, why? I will tell you why. She tells us stuff that disturbs us, she tells us things we can't imagine, tells us things we don't expect to hear, she tells us stuff that shocks us.

We expect to hear a story of a half-dressed lower-class woman and a depraved man, we try to visualise what happened, but the visual is two dimensional, it's dark, it only lasts 20 seconds, there's no sound, no movement as if no one was involved. When a woman tells her story of sexual abuse, it lasts longer than 20 seconds, we hear things we can't understand or accept and then doubts, suspicions and questions pore in, this makes us feel bad we protect ourselves from the discomfort.

There are two ways we typically use to protect ourselves from the discomfort, we either turn the volume up on the parts of the story we expect to hear and the volume down on the parts we don't expect to hear. We do this so we can believe her, so we can feel confident she is really a victim, however, this in itself is victimisation of the victim. It is victimisation because to believe she's innocent we need to think of her as paralysed, helpless and mute.

Or we do the exact opposite, we turn up the volume up on the things we don't expect to hear, the things we don't want to hear, and we turn the volume down on the things we expect to hear. We do this so we can hold on to doubts and feel more comfortable about them. Questions come up that aren't really questions, they are judgements.

Judgements that end with your verdict and the verdict is, she asked for it.

I have spoken out about my own taboo and painful topics in graphic detail as you know from reading this book and I personally believe this is the spark for change, change for ourselves in our healing and for society. And it forms part of the very reason I do the work I do and the purpose I have in my life, which is to make a difference in people's life's one beautiful person at a time.

We are forced to make difficult choices to survive sexual assault, let's make a call for all women and men to call out unacceptable behaviour and be leaders of change. Let's turn up the volume on all of it and prevent it from existing. Sexual abuse is often called a woman's issue, intrinsically a man's problem tied to definitions of manhood. This isn't just a woman's or a man's problem. It is a human issue, and we start to make the change we need by turning up the volume and speaking out, make the graphic details so loud that everyone will never be able to ignore it again. By making it undeniably present, and making it acceptable to speak the taboo. By taking away the silence, the taboo and the blame, I believe we can change the likelihood of it happening and be the change we all need to see.

Speak out, be loud, be the change.

I don't know you yet, but I love you still.

# CHAPTER 16

## THE FRIENDSHIP I PAID FOR DEARLY

A friendship that lasted almost a decade and not one I ever thought would end, however, it did. It was, as far as I believed, as close and as deep as any friendship could be. A sisterhood, divine family as I would say, let's name her Dorris. I'm choosing Dorris as a name because I imagine her as the type of person you would never expect to hurt you to your core. Just as I never expected to be hurt by her.

I held this friendship close to my heart and in a lot of ways didn't feel like I needed any other associations. Some would say that very naively I didn't put energy into other bonds. Dorris was a friend I even put above myself in many ways. I held Dorris in such high regard; I thought she was better than me, more successful than me, more focused than me. Dorris was at the birth of my daughter, and I invited her to every special occasion, celebration, business event and everything in between. She was a bridesmaid at my wedding in Barbados, and godmother to my daughter. We had a friendship I thought was ride or die. I did things for her like loan her money so

MICHELLE MARGARET MARQUES

she could take opportunities to grow her business, and I would put my plans on hold. I loaned her money to publish her book, which became a number one bestseller on Amazon. While I put my own on hold, hell I even paid for the writing course we both did. I would loan her cash from my bank account and then have to put things I needed on credit cards. I did everything for her, things I didn't even do for myself. I would pay for trips, pay for treats, pay for dinners and wine. When she visited me, I would give her free products from my spa, free treatments in my day spa, and when I visited her, I brought her products and wine. Our friendship had always been long distance. We met through an online networking group when I lived in Milton Keynes, and she lived in Somerset. We just hit it off immediately; it was like finding a missing piece of myself. We would talk for hours and hours. Every year in early January, we would go away for a couple of days and plan our year. Plan what we wanted for the next year of our personal life and business, of course, I paid for those trips (giggles)

In early 2017 after some serious encouragement from Dorris, I moved closer to her and moved into a house in Wiltshire. As I was on my own up in Cambridgeshire, she felt I had more of a network and support nearer to her. So, I leapt and moved in June 2017. In truth, I wasn't so sure about moving there at first, however, when I found the new place and I fully committed to the move, I was excited. We were going to set up a business together, one that I had put the concept together for some years earlier. We had been talking about setting it up for about three years at that point. I poured everything I had into the move and set up that business. We visited a health conference in Las Vagas August 2017 together. And I had made other loans to her. Dorris did not invest anything financially. After returning from Las Vagas, I didn't see her or hear from her much for almost a month. She kept putting things on hold to concentrate on her projects.

Meanwhile, I was now beginning to run into financial issues, and she kept putting things on hold. Things got so bad for me financially that I was having problems with my rent, and my landlord began eviction against me. Happily, I managed to resolve this. However, she still sat back without paying any of her debt or starting the business I'd paid to set up.

Things got so tricky with my finances, and everything seemed to hit at one time. My car needed a standard service, and I decided to get the MOT done at the same time. Suddenly my vehicle required significant and costly repairs, and it was off the road for three weeks. I lost a lot of money through another business transaction that didn't work out. Plus I had poured everything else into our new business, and I couldn't even afford to heat my house. My house was an old cottage surrounded by farmland, and we had oil heating. I didn't have enough to get the minimum tank order of oil. Dorris didn't even offer to get some of the money she owed me for me to heat my house for the winter. Dorris would come to visit, when I picked her up, of course, eat the food, and drink wine I bought. Then comment on how it was so cold you could see your breath in the kitchen. Still didn't even pay me £10 of the thousands she owed me or bring the wine for that matter.

My daughter and I spent the entire winter pf 2017/2018 with no central heating, living with fan heaters in the front room and 1 bedroom only just to stay warm together. To add to all of my financial issues. I spent the whole of Christmas and New Year alone in my freezing house, I didn't see her once, not even for an hour, in fact, I had barely seen her since getting back from Vegas. So much for all of the encouragement to move, where she was telling me to relocate down there. You have me here, you have Mum here (her mum) you have my sister, you have all the support you need here, more than what you have now. So much for that when I didn't even see her, not for one hour, because she told me she was so busy with her family. I thought I was family? I ended up being and certainly feeling more alone than I had ever felt, and I had the lowest time I had, had for many years.

In January 2018, I began to question myself, why I would allow anyone to treat me this way let alone one of the closest people in the world to me. I started wondering why I would put myself through such hardship for someone that certainly would not do the same for me. She knew I was alone in a freezing house and she didn't even invite me to hers for one hour, let alone visit me for an hour. I kept asking myself why I don't put myself ahead of her and why I had been more than happy in the past to put myself aside for her. I asked her the same questions in all honesty, and she didn't really give a response, except I always give and give to everyone, including her. I decided that enough was enough, I decided that I was going to focus on myself and above all absolutely and definitely put myself first. I decided that I was never going to put anything I wanted on hold again. I was going to move forward into 2018 focused on what I wanted and only what I wanted. The beginning of every year is always about letting go of what isn't working. And planning what I want to get out of the year ahead. I'm actually thankful that the last four months of 2017 were so severe and miserable. I realised I needed to be alone, I certainly needed to feel so very alone. I needed to feel so so isolated that I became so comfortable being alone. The only person I could think about on concentrate on was me. That is the lesson the universe needed and wanted me to learn. I needed to be so alone because little did, I know I was about to be Alone entirely and who knew it would be one of the most unexpected and heartbreaking ways to lose a friendship ever. However, it turned out to be one of the best things that could have ever happened to me. You see something happened inside me during that period of living in the cold and feeling alone, believe me, that is a combination of two of the things I dislike the most.

Something magical happened inside me, I realised I needed to love myself more. I didn't have enough love for myself, I had gone back to those old habits from before, just like I did in all of those failed relationships. Where I always gave and gave and gave, you know the ones where you think. If I just give more, if I'm just more tolerant if I can only be more loving and understanding If I just give more of myself if I can be more accepting, if I just do more, be more supportive. If I only show up willing and generous every time. If I just keep being a better person and an excellent friend, and I just do whatever I can. If I just give and give and give and give, at some point, somehow, I will get back what I deserve.

You see, life doesn't work like that, not when you are in that cycle. Life has givers, and takers and givers will give, and takers will take. We are all broken in some way, the only choice we have to make is if we want to stay broken or if we want to heal ourselves. The best thing that can ever happen to you is when you hit so low, and you feel so alone that you can only think about how you are going to take care of yourself and how you are going to get your ass in gear and really truly heal your heart and heal your bloody self. I've always had my fighter, she never leaves me ever, not really, she just lets me learn the hard way sometimes. Oh, but trust me, she always comes out fighting, because my Mother never put me on this earth to waste one bloody minute of this precious life. Let alone not use this big heart, not loving myself, healing myself and putting myself fucking first. I decided to move forward with that business, and I removed Dorris from the company directorship, and she wasn't exactly bothered about I have to say. I began to ask Dorris for my money. Dorris told me she couldn't pay me any money. However, instead of my usual, don't worry, I can wait. And the open heart, and smile type of attitude, Dorris was all too accustomed to by this time. I said no I'm afraid you have to find a way and at least begin to pay a minimum monthly sum.

You see not only was self-love and putting self-first coming into play in my world so prominently at that point, but the principle was also always at the forefront for me and always will be. Let me explain, the agreement between Dorris and I had always been that as long as I didn't need the money. I was happy to wait; however, if I ever found myself in the position where I needed it (YOU KNOW LIKE NOW, giggles), she would get it for me somehow. A fact I reminded her of instead of ahh ok I'll wait for it routine she had become used to. She proceeded to tell me, she couldn't pay me anything, not even the £300 per month that I had asked her to commit to, I know I hear you gasp and believe me I did more than gasp at this point. I was livid, to tell the truth, absolutely livid. I could not accept the sheer audacity when Dorris proceeded to say to me that she would have to wait until she was more comfortable before she could pay me, and that was likely to be May. Oh, I have to tell you this set such a fire inside me not just because of what she said. Because I now knew I was going to put myself first no matter what and I told her that I would not accept that. She would have to begin making payments because I had priorities, and they could not wait. I would not take it, how dare she treat me in such a way, how dare I ever accept anything that wasn't serving me again. I insisted she pay and guess what happened next? She dropped my ass as fast and as heartlessly as you can possibly imagine, let me just paint the picture for you. All of this communication happened via email. Not once did she come to see me or speak to me in person. Then I found myself blocked from, not only her Facebook but a group we were in, I realised I wasn't getting the notifications so I emailed her and she point-blank told me she felt it was best she removed me. What a punch in the gut. Bearing in mind, we hadn't had a discussion let alone a heated argument, best to remove me, what?

Then, as if this whole situation couldn't get more hurtful, I saw her at a networking group that we both attended monthly and where everyone knew we were not only business partners but also friends. Despite the issues, I wasn't going to treat her any different than my friend. I went over to say hello, and I leaned over to hug her, she barely lifted one arm half-heartedly and immediately turned and continued the conversation she was having. She ignored me the remainder of the night, oh and before I forget my daughter, who was six at that time was actually with me. Apart from an awkward goodbye where she sheepishly told me she would speak to me about things another time, when she found herself dead in front of me as I was struggling to leave after my daughter had fallen asleep and I had, had to go get my car from a nearby carpark while a practical stranger looked after my daughter. We never did speak in person again, not because I wasn't open to it, she never talked to me in person. Although she happily tore me apart in emails telling me I had clearly never valued the time she had given me or the advice she had given me, or when she had looked after me when I had an operation, or when she helped me unpack when I moved to my house in Wiltshire. I knew the value of all of that, I live in gratitude always and I am thanking for even the tiniest thing anyone does for me, because to me it is still valued, and it means the world to me and you can ask any one of my friends they will tell you I thank them for everything and I always bloody cry, they are used to it though as by now I'm sure you are too (smiling)  Although I found it interesting that she was suddenly reeling off the things she did for me, it didn't matter, because one, no matter what I knew I had given more of myself to that friendship and whatever way you looked at it I had paid for it, and two, I left that networking event that night knowing I would never allow that friendship back in my life again. I was so hurt; I sobbed all the way home and most of the night; I was embarrassed, and I was so angry at myself. Mad that I had accepted so little for so long.

My daughter asked me the next morning why Auntie Dorris didn't speak to us, and I just made an excuse that she was just busy. We never talked about Auntie Dorris again, and my daughter doesn't even ask me about her, they say children just know, who they should feel close to and who they shouldn't, and the truth is she was never really that close to Aunt Dorris, which I'm very grateful for now. It would have made the whole situation 100 times worse had I had to deal with her loss as well as my own perceived loss. As I write this book, one year on I still haven't received all of the money she owes, sure I've had dibs and drabs here and there, because I'm like a rottweiler when a principle is involved, I just lock on and don't let go. She actually made a comment at one point that she had no doubt I would pursue her for the money because she had seen me go after other people for a lot less and she is actually right. I may be big-hearted, giving, loving and kind, but I'm not letting go of the principles I stand by for nothing and no one.

I was blindsided by what happened in this situation, and I beat myself up severely and repeatedly for not seeing it coming. How could a highly intelligent, strong, suffer no fools, take no shit woman let this happen? How could I not see it coming and from the person that was closest in my world, there is the answer right there, I involved her the most in my world, I trusted her implicitly, I would have trusted her with my beating heart in her hand if I was dying on the floor. The way that friendship ended fed right into all of my deepest darkest fears. I was never enough, never important enough, and it felt like I was dropped in the trash like a piece of paper that was no longer useful. I was so hurt, I stayed alone practically wholly shut off from everyone for another 8 months just working and taking care of my daughter. Rebuilding myself and my life, I didn't want anyone close to me again. I felt so betrayed and used, but the truth is whatever hurt I felt, and whatever was or wasn't at play in that friendship I was a willing participant and I take full responsibility for all of the pain and everything I gave to that friendship be it love, money, time or unwavering support and I know now I haven't lost anything I wasn't meant to lose, it too shall pass. I was meant to go through that because I was meant to learn to be really alone, because when you have been really isolated, and you have become so comfortable with being alone can you really truly find yourself, find your inner strength, find your inner peace and absolutely, and ultimately connect with your self-love in a way that you never imagined possible. Something magical happened in those 12 months, the four prior and most certainly the 8 that followed, because we were now headed to another time of the year that is always about rebirth for me, in fact, I actually view it as my new year because of course, it is, it's my birthday. I've always used October as a time for reflection and making plans, and October 2018 was no different in that respect. However, the difference was how deep and profound the thought was and how strong the desire was for total rebirth, a complete transformation. The exact same metamorphism of a butterfly coming out of its cocoon, I needed to go out of mine. I wanted so badly to get back to my life fully, and I knew that the only way I could do this was to completely unpick everything and transform every relationship or situation in my life that simply wasn't working for me anymore. So, I set out on a journey that would transform everything in my life as I know it then and has transformed me in ways I could never imagine.

That transformation will take me on the journey of a lifetime, and you will find out in the next chapter what that journey is, but for now all I want you to do, hmm she says all, I want you to do (smile) is to look at what relationships are not serving you, what needs to change in order for you to really connect with you and what you deserve, what metamorphism is absolutely necessary for you to live the life you are genuinely in love with. What decisions do you want to take that ensures your love for yourself is always the strongest and is still first.

Through the most profound betrayal I could ever imagine, I found the deepest love I could ever imagine, for myself! I hope you don't have to go through any betrayal at all before you tap into the most profound love and respect for yourself. When you have that level of love for yourself, first of all, you will only attract people with the capacity to love on the same level, and no one can ever hurt you so deeply again.

# CHAPTER 17

## MY SON STEPHEN

My firstborn, Stephen (spelt the Scottish way of course) it was important to me that it was Scottish. Wow, I never thought I could feel such love. It's not the kind of love that builds no this love just hits you all at once like a steam train running right over the top of you. It's the best feeling in the world and the scariest. He was perfect, oh my goodness, piercing blue eyes that looked right through my soul. I just wanted to love him, hold him forever and never let him go. I couldn't believe I had done that, I had produced such a perfect and healthy human being. How my life changed forever that day in so many beautiful and challenging ways and although I could never have known the reality of the responsibility ahead of me, I wouldn't have changed it for the world. Now I had my, little man I could love unconditionally and that is an extraordinary gift.

He was a good baby, he never really cried, he slept right through the night most of the time from day one, I used to have to wake him up to feed him. He slept so much I used to nudge him to make sure he was still alive and check that he was breathing.

Sometimes I would just sit and watch him sleep, he was just so beautiful, and all I wanted to do was love him and give him the world. I felt like the luckiest Mum in the world. Stephen has always had a great character, he's utterly charming, he has this shy like, smile but with a total glint in his eyes. He has this endearing giggle when he gets embarrassed, and he gets really flushed. Always full of life, smiling, and talking too, talks a lot and asks about everything. He is bold and loud (wonder where he gets that from), he loves life and my gosh he's so intelligent.

He was spoiled, first son, first grandson on both sides and first great-grandson too. A lot of first's and a lot of people wanting to give him all the attention and love they could. But all I wanted was to have him to myself, the end of the day was the best time when it was just him and I, and I got to snuggle with him and just talk to him, those times were so precious.

He had a rough start, not the beginning I wanted him to have by any means. The rocky relationship with his father and the tension in our house. He was a happy baby despite that because he was surrounded by love. The things that happened with his father when he was just six months old and us splitting up. I really did have him all to myself then, for the most part anyway. My Mum was there every day, but at night and in the mornings it was just him and I. Mum looked after him while I went to college.

After my Mum died he came back with me full time, and I don't think either of us coped with it very well for a while, but we found our way eventually. He was too young to understand why my Mum wasn't there anymore, but I know it affected him still and he missed her.

He could be challenging to handle at times, but deep down, he is such a sweet soul. Very loving and caring, but he will do things his way make no mistake about that (umm just like me, giggle). We have always had the kind of relationship that was very good one minute where he would talk to me about anything and share laughs and jokes, then the next we would be in battle, I was hell-bent on him doing things my way, and he was hell-bent on doing them his way for sure. It was like a war zone in my house sometimes. I loved him regardless, and despite the battles, he always told me he loved me when all was said and done. His friends were at our house a lot, I was the cool Mum as far as they were concerned, although he always protested about that opinion.

He didn't like the word, no (in fact he still doesn't) and he really didn't want to follow the rules.

We always worked it out though, I couldn't stay mad at him with that charming smile and those eyes beaming at me. He is a fantastic person, with so much to offer the world and so handsome, oh my goodness those eyes just get bluer and more piercing. Always wants to have fun, always joking around and that laugh of his is just so infectious (makes me giggle just thinking about it) and when he laughs his whole face just shines. Whenever we go out anywhere, people often assume he's my boyfriend or, ask him if I'm his girlfriend, he always answers very firmly with no that's my mother. He gets very embarrassed his cheeks get very flushed, and I just think it's funny (it's a significant ego boost for me right). The best thing about having his so young. I do think a lot of the ups and downs we have is partly because I was so young, we are like friends, I was still growing up while he was growing up. I didn't always get it right, but it wasn't without trying and having his best interests at heart. He does tell me everything at times (sometimes too much), and we have a great connection when we do get along. When we don't get along oh boy it's fierce, but he's also fiercely protective of me when it comes to anyone else disrespecting me. We are very alike, very stubborn, very vocal, very passionate, immensely loving and at times, very sensitive. It makes for a great relationship and an explosive one in equal measure, but it all comes back to love.

I'm excited about the future, I'm so looking forward to seeing what he achieves and how he grows as a man. He isn't a dad yet, but I hope he becomes one because he would be an amazing dad. His spirit of fun and love are amazing qualities for a child to grow up with, he would be strict but fair, and I do know he really wants to be a dad. I am so proud of him, and I love him just as much now as I always have from that first day. I have so much love for him, it sometimes just boils over, when I look at him smiling with that cheeky glint in his eyes I just burst with love and pride. He has brought me so much joy and some heartache. Even although we still have our ups and downs from time to time and again slip back on to the battlefield, he will always be my baby boy, my firstborn, my first real true love and his eyes will always have my soul.

Stephen baby, I have all the love in the world for you. Just love, nothing but love.

Love Mum xx

I don't know you, yet, but I love you still.

# CHAPTER 18

## MY SON MICHAEL

My second baby boy, Michael, named after me, of course (smile). There was that rush of love all over again, as a mother the capacity we have for love just amazes me still today. It's wasn't quite the same steam train just hitting me this time perhaps because I knew what to expect but even the same amount of love. He was beautiful, of course, as I knew he would be after having my first beautiful son (giggle). He was like a chubby little sumo wrestler weighing in at 10 lbs and 4 ounces when he was born, he was like a giant baby, and he certainly didn't look like a newborn. Cute chubby cheeks, wrists, knees, and ankles that were just adorable. Big brown eyes, like pools you could see yourself in, and I just wanted to love him forever.

Micheal was also a good baby, although he didn't sleep as much as Stephen and he definitely loved his food, I never had to wake him up for a feed that's for sure. He was calm and content, and he still is now. He has a very mild nature, loving and quiet, the complete opposite of Stephen. Michael is a thinker, he is efficient in his thinking, and he loves to learn everything he can. Our relationship was always close, he was definitely a Mummies boy. Michael liked to please and follow the rules, something that didn't go down well with Stephen; he called him the golden boy. There's no golden boy for me though, they are just very different people, and I love them just as much because of their differences and characters. Michael was less confident growing up, he didn't go out much he liked to be at home. He is very laid back, very accepting just goes with the flow, but rub him up the wrong way, and he will let you know your place (umm wonder where he gets that from) directly but quietly and calmly. He would talk to me about everything in his life, and we would talk for hours sometimes, always full of ideas. He is highly intelligent and very focused, sometimes quite single-mindedly. He is so kind and gentle, and he has a big broad smile, although he liked to look moody most of the time, oh boy he had such a serious look, and he still does. He has such a calm, soothing voice, he used to work on my reception in my salon and customers always praised how professional he sounded and could never believe he was my 17-year-old son. He had a much more serious attitude and a very responsible approach to everything. Never got in trouble and always got good grades, he was like the dream child I never had to worry about and in a lot of ways blended into the background.

Michael left home at 18 under not so amicable circumstances which, was a complete shock to me at the time, I would never have expected that and we lost our relationship. I am still heartbroken today, tears fill my eyes right now. We do speak now, but it is a long, long way from the relationship I would desperately love to have and there is a big chunk of missed time that I can never get back, but I remain hopeful for the future. He is a dad, and I am beyond proud of the dad he is, he works a full-time job over three and a half days, and he looks after my grandaughter the other three and a half days because he is no longer with her mother. Despite the circumstances, I like to think he is the parent he is today because of the way I raised him. I always knew Michael would be an amazing dad, but how he steps up as a man blows me away. He is adamant that she is his full responsibility and he takes care of not just her 50/50 but all of her financial needs too.

He has told me that he found it difficult at times, growing up around my dysfunctional family. And when he became a father, he made a choice that he never wanted my granddaughter to grow up around that influence and so he decided to keep her away from my family, including me. He said he kept her away from me just so my family could never be involved. Despite the fact that the difficulties we all suffered were as a result of other people's lifestyles and choices within my family, and my own decisions. I desperately tried as much as possible to keep my sons as far away from the influences as I could at the time and did my best to give them a healthy home life. I do understand that it wasn't always the best situation to grow up in, and I absolutely agree that my grandaughter should not have that in her life. I would dearly love for Michael to understand I did my best with the situation I found myself in, and if I could turn back time, I would have moved them away entirely too. In fact, I did run several times for that very reason, I also was always trying to get away from it, it just followed me every time. Until we finally moved far enough away, but by then the effects had left their scar on us all. I didn't know just how affected Michael was by these things, I knew he never liked the drama. My family continuously brought chaos into our lives, and it always affected him more than Stephen. However, it was only a few years ago when he told me exactly how much it affected him and how he felt about keeping my granddaughter away. It breaks my heart to know how much he was affected. However, I believe it did teach him to have the courage to change things for his family, and I am very proud of that, he is an amazing dad, and I agree wholeheartedly with his choice.

I just hope that Michael can find it in his heart to understand I did the best I could at the time, and I always had my sons best interests at heart. I never set out to chose that lifestyle, but I do take responsibility for how it affected him. I think the kind of person and father he is, speaks volumes about who he is inside, but I also think it speaks volumes of the actual influence I was on his life, the kind of mother I am and the kind of grandmother I could be. I've always taught my children to aim high and achieve, I've always encouraged all of them to dream and think big. I have always told them all, they can do anything they put their mind to, and I just want to be that influence in my granddaughter's life too. I would give anything to work on putting it behind us and rebuilding our relationship. I love you, please come back to me.

Michael is my beautiful calming influence, and I love him so much, he is a fantastic person that I am so proud of. I am hopeful for the future, and I know he will achieve incredible things, but I'm excited to see how much more he grows as a man. He is the best dad, and I cannot express how that makes me feel as a mother.

Michael baby I have all the love in the world for you. Just love, nothing but love.

Love Mum xx

I don't know you, yet, but I love you still.

# CHAPTER 19

## MY SON LIAM

My third born, and what a little delight. The same volume of love I had experienced before came flooding through my heart. With each birth, I had more love in my life and more love in my heart. I just never imagined the capacity we have for love as Mother's.

Liam was just a bundle of absolute joy, never very demanding. A very laid back personality, sometimes too laid back. He's a very loving person, and when he was little, he liked to be helpful. Always affectionate, loved nothing more than a good hug and lots of attention. I would say he was probably the most loving of the boys, although they were all loving in their own ways. We went through a difficult time with Liam's Grandmother. Who decided she wanted custody of him, and after a long, painful and very stressful battle, I lost full custody of him. This was very difficult for me, I missed him terribly. However, it did give us a unique relationship and bond. We talked a lot whenever it was possible, and when he was with me, I just gave him all of my attention and love. I probably overcompensated way too much, because of the guilt I felt for him not being with his brothers and me all the time. And in many ways spoiled him and let him get away with more than he should have.

We have always had a good relationship, and despite some bumps along the way we still do now. I don't think we can ever expect any relationship to be problem-free. Especially, ones with our children and I've had many conversations with women who have very similar stories.

Liam is a highly intelligent person, and I love the conversations that we have. We have some really intellectual discussions, he is very passionate about the world we live in. The environment and human suffering are his most significant concerns. He is very vocal and very opinionated, straight forward and not afraid to go against the grain. His knowledge and viewpoint blow me away at times, he never ceases to amaze me that's for sure. He is his own person, something I really admire about him. He doesn't care what anyone thinks of him or what he thinks, he is very comfortable with who he is, and I'm very proud of that. He has dreadlocks, wears ethical clothing and is very mindful of what he eats. I guess you could say he's a bit of a modern-day hippy (giggle). He is such a gentle soul, however, make no mistake he can turn on you if you attempt to abuse him. He's like a gentle giant, a soft soul with a calm demeanor until he's not if that makes sense.

I love him so very deeply, and I miss him so much. I am so looking forward to watching him grow and witnessing the difference he will make in this world, although he's still finding himself and his purpose right now. I have no doubt that he will accomplish amazing things, his passion is so great, and when he channels it in the right direction, it will be so powerful. I'm not sure if he wants to be a dad; however, I know he would be an amazing one. I look forward to his future, whatever that might be.

Liam baby, I have all the love in the world for you. Just love, nothing but love.

Love Mum xx

I don't know you, yet, but I love you still.

# CHAPTER 20

## MY DAUGHTER

I always wanted a girl every time I got pregnant, and it was no secret. I wanted to have the same relationship I had with my Mum with her. As you know, I believe I manifested her in my life.

My pregnancy with her is the only one where I found out the sex and went for private scans. As soon as I reached sixteen weeks in my pregnancy, I had a scan to find out the sex. I could see very; clearly, she was a girl I just couldn't believe my eyes. After almost twenty-two years, I was finally getting my girl, and I would wait another twenty-two years; she is so worth the wait. The ultrasound technician said you know what it is right, and I blurted out no in a panic of doubt. She said it's a girl, you are having a girl. I just started sobbing uncontrollably, the woman didn't know what to do. She asked as she clutched her chest in a worried way, are you ok, is that good or bad. I managed to string together in between still sobbing you don't know how good this is. She had a sigh of relief and said you had me worried, we both laughed. I left her office, went straight to a baby store and bought a pink rabbit, I was so happy I don't think I stopped smiling for the entire pregnancy. That night I went for a soak in the bath, and as I went, I told her dad I'm going to spend some quality time with my daughter (smile). I stayed in that bath for a long time. Singing loudly and, replying Make you feel my love by Adele over and over again. From that moment on, my life became all about making her feel my love. Having quality time with my daughter. And building a relationship with her that will be strong until my last breath.

Let me actually tell you about her now. She is the most caring, kind and loving person that could have ever blessed my life. She blows my mind with how intelligent she is. Her compassion and understanding of others are awe-inspiring. The love I receive from her fills me up every single day. The love I feel when I hold her just makes my heart burst. We have a bond that is unbreakable and very special. Our energy is very much in-sink, we just completely understand each other. I absolutely adore spending time with her, and it really doesn't matter what we are doing. We have so much fun, and the conversations are just beautiful. She is a little powerhouse, she knows her own mind, and she isn't afraid to tell you how she feels. (wonder where she gets that from, giggle). She is her mother's daughter make no mistake about that (smile). She is stunning, she has such beauty inside and out, and every time I look at her, my heart just melts with pride. She is my heart, my soul and my life.

I'm very open with her, and I consult her about what she thinks before I make many decisions, including business decisions. She is confident, polite, incredibly well behaved and elegant. She can hold a conversation in any situation, and I never have to worry about taking her anywhere. She is a part of everything I do, she comes to events and meetings with me. Her middle name forms part of my skincare brand and will become the brand name for my children's range. We are a team, and she is my little hero. She has healed me in many ways and made me want to show up differently in this world.

I often say if I had her first, I wouldn't have had any more children, and it's also the reason I will never have more. That has nothing to do with the love I have for my sons, I wouldn't change having them for the world. However, I do love the dynamic I have with just her and me now. A mother-daughter love is very different from that of a mother and son, my entire existence is now worthwhile. My life is so very complete. I am beyond excited to see the amazing woman I know without a doubt, she will become, and I cannot wait to see everything she achieves in her life. Look out world!

CC baby, I have all the love in the world for you. Just love, nothing but love.

Love Mummy xx

I don't know you, yet, but I love you still.

# CHAPTER 21

## RAISING FOUR CHILDREN ALONE

Seems to be a cycle for me, and I can tell you one that I am personally quite happy with for the most part, especially now. I love standing on my own two feet and doing things for myself. It gives me a sense of pride and strength, and you get to know yourself well. It wasn't always that way though; there have been times in my life that I have found it extremely difficult and times when I have thrived in it. I'm going to split this chapter into two distinct parts, and you will notice where I wasn't coping and where I was succeeding.

I raised my boys alone for almost thirteen years, and for the most part, I did well on my own. Times, where I didn't do well, was when my life was in chaos and that usually had something to do with my fucked up family or lack of money. I didn't do well in either of these two situations. The chaos with my family always had an impact on me emotionally, mainly due to me holding on to the latest incident and allowing myself to be a victim of it, although at the time I never realised that. There are obvious reasons for that, as you already know from the bits and pieces you have learned about my family background. Let me explain more about the chaos lack of money caused me. Lack of cash threw me into complete turmoil inside; I would obsess over having enough money. I had this drive to provide more for my boys than was possible at times or more than I needed to for sure.

I was obsessed with having more, doing better, giving everything I could to them, and giving them experiences of the world that would allow them to see how much they could achieve. I put myself through a lot in the process and them at times, let me tell you. I was so driven by wanting to have a perfect life, and giving them more; I was often blind to the mistakes I was making. I made a lot of errors, and although they came from the best intentions, they also caused a lot of stress and upheaval at times too. I did whatever it sometimes took to provide for my sons; I often overextended my finances to make our life better. I couldn't see that sometimes it didn't make our life better at all. I thought as long as I kept going stayed strong and as long as I fixed whichever mistake I made and never gave up, it was ok. Sure they are good assets to have in your back pocket, but the damage was done regardless. Our life was a balance of fantastic experiences and stressful shitty mistakes. Mistakes that cost me my home on several occasions, because we lived in-expensive houses in good neighbourhoods and I couldn't juggle finances all the time. I thought I was doing the right thing; I thought I could make it work every time. We travelled to a lot of countries, holidays that I really couldn't afford on reflection, but I wanted my sons to have what I didn't have growing up. I wanted them to see the world and know the world was a wondrous place. I wanted to expand their minds and their experience of life. In doing this, I put myself under constant stress and them in situations they shouldn't have had to deal with sometimes. I couldn't see that if I just took a step back and rained a few things in, we would have been better overall. I was so caught up in giving them everything I could, and I didn't care what I had to put myself through to do it. I did whatever it took, not just to survive and have a decent life; I did whatever it took to have the best of life, including some very questionable and illegal choices at times. There were a few incidents where I was offered the opportunity to use credit cards that had been obtained in other peoples names. I didn't personally apply for the cards, and I'm not excusing my actions either. I took the opportunity to use them. Some people I knew who were in the business of fraud needed a female who looked respectable enough to use the cards. They got what they wanted from each of the cards, and I got what I wanted too.

I took my son's shopping and let them get whatever they wanted. I also deposited false checks in to two of my bank accounts, withdrew the money and then closed the account before the check bounced. I can't tell you how they got the checks or how the scam worked. I do know I was so driven to maintain our lifestyle that I even resorted to things I'm not proud of at all. As much as we lived in a good neighbourhood and my sons went to school with friends who's parents were lawyers and doctors I was a single Mum struggling to get by and I was acquainted with the kind of contacts that gave me a-way sometimes to take the pressure off or to give my boys more whichever was the driving force at the time. Coupled with my constant drive to give my sons a life to rival their friends, lack of money caused such anxiety and turmoil in me that I had to do just about anything I could to calm it. I didn't have anyone I could go to for help with money; in fact, everyone else always came to me, which was an added factor. It doesn't sound like I had any boundaries at all; however, I did have some I never stole from anyone personally, and there were many things I would not involve myself in that I could have easily gotten myself into, such as selling drugs which were offered to me multiple times. As I've said, I'm not proud of what I did, and I take full responsibility for my actions. I've been harder on myself over the years than anyone else could be, and I repeatedly beat myself up for my choices. I wasn't proud of the reflection looking at me in the mirror no matter how hard I tried or how good I thought my intentions were, and I knew I had to change it. I am proud of who I am now and if you ask me would I have made the same choices again if I could go back, and I will tell you yes I probably would, because I was dealing with circumstances I often couldn't cope with and I was doing my best at that time with what I had. Ask me if I wish I had learned my mistakes much sooner and found a way out of my cycle quicker, and I will tell you hell, yes. I can't change any of it; all I can do is learn and make better choices of who I want to be in this world and how I want to show up. It sounds harsh, but I've done enough apologising and proving, I've done the work it has taken to make peace with who I was then and the consequences my choices had. I don't justify any of it, and I used to be very ashamed of it. I carried a lot of guilt for a long time. But the bottom line is, it is what it is, they are choices I made, and I stand in my truth.

The contrast in my truth now is that my life is far removed from that stressful, chaotic life. It's just my daughter and me now, I've learned to curb the drive to provide so much that I put us in unnecessary situations. My life is improved dramatically, not because I'm a better person or a better mother either, because my circumstances are very different, and I have learned from my past mistakes. I also only have one child to take care of, which makes life so much easier. My drive is balanced, between having more and what is obtainable with finances available. I don't overextend financial obligations, and in many ways, I live a much more simple life. I'm able to do this because I've come through the complexities of life, and I have worked on myself enough to know what is essential and what is not. I no longer need the feel-good factor that a lot of my financial decisions were born from before. I didn't love myself back then, and I sure as hell wasn't proud of my choices. I have learned to love myself deeply now and accept the dark and the light, and I can tell you that was a key element and a massive turning point. I learned that it is far more valuable to have a stressfree, simple, loving and joyful life than to have all of the most valuable things in this world. I can raise my daughter now the way I always wanted to raise my sons. I am thankful that I made my mistakes and I am grateful I have been able to learn enough from them to know how to bring her up in a stable environment, based on love and encouragement to achieve. I never forget that my circumstances are very different now, and I don't take away any of the responsibility for all of the pain I caused my sons. However, I do take credit for always trying, never giving up, continuously growing and still having the best intentions at heart; however misguided my path to getting there was.

I love life now, and I love being a mother. I feel validated for all that I have achieved against all the odds and mistakes. I feel excited for all that has passed and for what is to come. I feel proud of who I have become and how I show up in the world today. I am thankful for everything positive and negative in my life. The strength of character it has given me, for all of the lessons and the person, it all helped mould. I am ride or die, I will never give up, and I will continuously grow and develop myself. I've never lost sight of the bigger picture, and I'm well on my way to achieving everything I ever dreamed of doing.

I have fucked up big time, I have learned, and I have adjusted my actions accordingly. I can never change the past, but I can change the future. I put all my fucking energy into doing better now; my drive is to give back and make a difference with my lessons. Take ownership of your shit, believe me, its the best thing you will ever do for yourself and everyone else.

I don't know you, yet, but I love you still.

# CHAPTER 22

## NOT KNOWING MY GRANDAUGHTER FROM BIRTH

I never in my life imagined that I would find myself in the position of not sharing in the joy of having a grandchild, especially with my son Michael. Growing up Michael and I were always close, he was with me all the time, he talked to me about everything, he also worked in the reception of my salon. I thought we would be close forever.

Until one day quite literally he wasn't there, I woke up to find my front door to the house slightly open and him, gone along with all of his things. There had been a lot of tension between us regarding his girlfriend at the time, my Grandaughter's mother. We didn't see eye to eye, but I never imagined he would just leave like that. I went after him of course, and I didn't correctly behave the way I should have, I was out of my mind actually. He never spoke to me for five years after that and things are still fractured even now. I admit I didn't approach the situation the right way; however, I don't believe I deserved that, no Mother who has given the best of her despite her mistakes does. I admit my mistakes, I accept full responsibility for them, and I've apologised, but I feel I lost way too much for those mistakes.

I can't explain what it's like to suddenly lose your son like that for me it was heartbreaking, you can't accept that a child you raised all alone and had tried your best to give everything to, just decided to cut you out of his life. As well as suddenly losing him, my other son Liam shared the news that I was going to be a Grandmother about a year after Michael left home. Finding out you are going to have a Grandchild is meant to be joyful and exciting, it's meant to be quite magical, especially for the first time. Planning to spoil them and shower them with love, all of the love my Mum gave my first son. The joy and explosion of love and emotion of holding them in your arms for the first time and watching them grow. I felt I had that taken away from me, and it was just more heartbreak, my heart was breaking so badly that I just shut it out and pretended it wasn't happening. Michael didn't tell me when she was born, and I wasn't allowed to go see her. I did contact him when I was given the news to congratulate him and tried to express that I hoped he would understand what the challenges of being a parent were like and how much you put into a child, he took it as offensive and shut me out once more.

I didn't see my Grandaughter until she was almost five years old, I have to express it was the strangest feeling. This beautiful little person that was part of me, yet a stranger, a child I didn't know at all. I wanted to hug her, squeeze her tight and tell her I love her, but she didn't know me, and I didn't know her. The first time I held my Grandaughter, it was a quick hug with my mind firmly focused on not making her feel uncomfortable. I was excited and nervous all at the same time, I was on eggshells the whole time, making sure I didn't say anything that would spoil the entire thing and get me cut out again. When we were saying our goodbyes I had to focus all of my, mind, on not breaking down like some crazy woman, this child didn't know. I haven't seen her since then either, I still tread very carefully with my son, sometimes he speaks to me and sometimes he doesn't. I send him messages without expectation now, I've learned it's too painful to do anything else.

I would dearly love to have a proper relationship with my Grandaughter, and I will never give up hope of recovering a good relationship with my son and making up for lost time with my Grandaughter.

For now, I just keep treading gently and making sure he knows I'm here and willing, that I love him and her and I always will no matter what happens. I will never give up my dream that one day, it will all be a distant memory, and we will all be together laughing and making memories.

Never give up on anyone you love, if it is worth fixing. Sometimes, it isn't worth repairing, and you have to be willing to see the difference.

I don't know you, yet, but I love you still.

# CHAPTER 23

## FATHER OR NOT

Does it matter or not? That's the question that keeps swirling around in my head right now, as I sit to write this chapter.

When I planned the book, I decided I was going to add this chapter about never really feeling my father cared for me or cared for much else for that matter. Then I began to question if it was really relevant or if it even deserved space. That's a bold statement that actually goes against how I choose to show up in this world. However, I am human, and I can't write a book about being authentic if I'm not fully prepared to be authentic. So perhaps this chapter is really about authenticity and accepting our dark and our light. It can also be said that writing this is really about seeing the dark and the light in my life as a whole. I received a lot of light from my mother for which I am forever grateful, and I have received a lot of dark from my father, for which I am thankful none the less. I guess it creates balance and a certain amount of self-awareness of my own dark and light. The experiences I have unpicked in my life and pieced back together.

I actually really see life as a series of experiences you unpick and learn from. And my relationship or lack thereof, with my father, is certainly something that has had a lot of unpicking. It's a strange experience to explain. My father was always around growing up, but he was never really around if that makes sense, in other words, he was certainly not present in the moment. After my mother passed away, my father never really gave any support in any way with grief, with my life, my sons when they were growing up, and now with my daughter. My daughter has only ever seen him three times briefly in her now eight years of life. He has never supported any of my business endeavours. In fact, he has actually always been negative and even against me creating my own business.

As far as love goes, this is something I never really ever felt from him growing up. I indeed haven't felt loved in my adulthood, and since my mother passed away. We only talk when I contact him, and I only see him if I go to his house, I do not get a birthday call, Christmas or New Year and my children don't get any care or support from him either. This is a relationship that, in the past, caused me a lot of pain and anger. I really had to work through some deep inner work on this one. It is a relationship that I had to make a choice to remove at least emotionally from my life and one I'm happy to say I have made my own peace with and have accepted it for what it is. It's no better or worse than it is, it just is.

I wanted to share this with you because, for a lot of years, I really tried to work at this relationship, and I caused myself a lot of pain in doing so. I felt angry that he doesn't love me or care about my life and it made me feel so very unimportant, that feeling of unimportance is a feeling that hung over me and resurfaced in many situations and that didn't serve me or my life one tiny bit. Those negative emotions caused a lot of pain in my life and affected a lot of my emotional wellbeing for a lot of years.

Those emotions affected other relationships and the way I dealt with any situation that triggered those emotions, those feelings of not being important and not feeling loved. Anger was always the emotion that was triggered, and I really didn't deal with it well, it still had a negative outcome.

If you have any kind of relationship in your life, especially a parental one that is negative and causes you so much pain or that you know is affecting other areas of your life deeply. I urge you to do the inner work you need to do to heal yourself and have the courage to choose to emotionally remove yourself. Love yourself first, I can honestly say I really wish I learned this so much earlier, my healing really took flight when I learned to fall deeply in love with myself, the dark and the light, and by accepting the dark I was really able to see just how beautiful the light is.

Acceptance of oneself and acceptance of others is the key.

I don't even know you, but I love you still. Smile and love yourself.

# CHAPTER 24

## ALWAYS FEELING ALONE

### And

### Discovering I Really Never Was

Pretty much my whole adult life I have felt alone in this world, it's no real surprise to me now looking back. I'm sure it won't be for you either once you understand what happened in my early years.

I know that stems from the childhood sexual abuse I suffered. Then almost dying at the age of 17 when my firstborn was just 6 months old. After being beaten by my, Son'd Father, a man that was meant to love and cherish me, and left unconscious with internal bleeding. And then add the significant losses I suffered early in my adult life. I lost my Grandmother, who was a very significant person in my life, two months before my 18th birthday. We were very close, there wasn't a day that passed where I didn't spend some time with my Grandmother. Until the last couple of months before she passed away because I just didn't know how to handle it. My Mother passed away 14 months after my Grandmother, only 10 days before my 19th birthday. My Mother and I were incredibly close, especially since having my Son and losing my Grandmother. She was the most important person in my life, aside from my young Son at that time.

By now, of course, you know all the details of my childhood sexual abuse. I promise you will learn the full stories of the beating that almost cost me my life. And the losses of both of these amazing women in their own chapters and the significant roles they played in the woman I am today.

For now, I'm going to concentrate on telling you how I caused myself so much heartache and pain. I did this by not dealing with my own emotional healing and just pretending to myself and the world around me. I was okay. And never really acknowledging to myself that I feared being left each time I got close to someone or let them into my world.

I now know I imposed a large amount of those feelings on myself and in some ways deep down I never really let anyone close enough to me for them to indeed be there for me. My friendships and relationships where generally with people who were mostly emotionally unavailable, a pattern it took me a long time to recognise.

My young adulthood was shadowed by a lot of pain, a lot of heartaches I really didn't know how to deal with, nor did I have a chance to really deal with it. I had just lost the two most important and significant women in my life, the two biggest influences I had ever had. Love and happiness seemed like it really wasn't meant for me. I was a 19-year-old single Mum, I had a two-year-old to take care of and a family that completely imploded after the death of my Mother. I had a lot of responsibility and not much else. It was a lot to handle, and I just did what I do best, get on with it.

Unconsciously I had chosen a path which meant I could feel secure, but not cared for or loved. I spent much of my adulthood giving and giving and giving to people who I failed to recognise I could never receive love or support properly from anyone. Because I was so damn focused on providing all the time in the hope, I would just get that same level in return. The problem was, the more I gave, the more I felt I wasn't getting enough back. Truth is no one could have ever given enough, or measured up to my giving. Because I didn't love myself enough to receive love properly from anyone or even to recognise it as enough love. The story I had learned or was certainly telling myself was that I wasn't meant to be loved properly, I wasn't good enough, I didn't deserve true happiness or a proper loving family. When I am close to people, they either really hurt me or leave me and if I just kept giving more love, more generosity, more understanding, more tolerance, more, more, more, we all know how the pattern goes. I would somehow become enough, and be worthy of love, be worthy of happiness and people in my life who were truly there for me. Of course, what happens is the complete opposite, because we are operating from such low vibrating energy that we don't attract the right people into our life in the first place. When I say right, I don't mean they are wrong in some way, they just aren't right for us in that energy, because they can't give you what you needed or need.

One big question I hear you ask yourself is how to break the cycle, or how I broke the cycle. It's actually effortless. Self-love, really truly finding love for who you are inside, falling deeply and madly in love with the beautifully incredible person you arc, including your unique edges and imperfections. Cherish and adore yourself more than you could ever need anyone else to. True acceptance of oneself and being completely unapologetically you. Once I learned to truly love myself and more importantly accept myself and really step into being all of me, my whole world opened up, and I literally began to see a whole new me. I actually started to see just how powerful, reliable and capable I am and how much capacity I have for loving other people deeply. You see self-love is not just about you, it's about everyone around you. When you love yourself enough, when you give yourself enough, when you know how important you are and how you show up in this world so deep down in your soul. No one can ever take it from you, your capacity to give to the world as a whole around you grows and grows with every act of love and kindness you give to yourself.

Although it may be one of the most challenging journeys of self-discovery, you will ever embark on. I can assure you it is worth it and will be your greatest love and greatest ally. Suddenly the world is brighter, the grass is a whole new shade of green, the sky is the most vivid blue even on a cloudy day, your step just springs for no reason at all, your hair always looks so bloody good, but most of all you just can't help but shine, shine, shine and spread love.

I encourage you to be loving, with everyone, even the stranger you meet on the street, however, I encourage you to be the most devoted being you can possibly be with yourself first and foremost, it will change your life in ways you can never have imagined was possible.

I don't know most of you yet, but I can promise you I already love you. You are loved and adored always, it's right there inside you xx.

I will let you in on a little secret, I felt a great deal of emotion writing this chapter, initially typing with tears running down my face. Lots of thoughts about my Mum whose picture is always on my desk and of course, of my Grandmother, not of grief exactly but in recognition of what amazing strong and inspiring women they were and how I wish I could have spent a lifetime with them. What amazing women my Sons and my Daughter missed out on knowing. However, the emotion is more strongly linked to the sincere gratitude that I have for the part they did play in my life and the influence they still have in my life, and my children's life's and the little signs of love and beauty I can see from them all around me.

Even although you were there for such a short time, your influence will outlive time. Love you, Mum. I Love you, Nana xxx. (There go the tears again, that's me, giggle)

# CHAPTER 25

## BEING STRONG AND FINDING STRENGTH IS THE SAME

To find strength and be strong is the same. You first need to be strong to find your strength, and you need strength to be strong.

I have learned in life that even seemingly strong people need to find strength and those who don't think they are strong have strength. We have it inside us, in fact, we have everything we need inside us we just have to have the power to access it.

People always ask me how I stay so strong, they say they couldn't have gone through half of what I've gone through, a third even. I suppose I have had to, I was meant to. My Mum always said what is meant for you will never go past you, and I know she did not in any way foresee the struggles I have had, but she was right. We get in life what is meant for us, in other words, what we attract the most. I have had a series of turbulence in my life that has meant I have had to be strong, and I am able to find more strength each time because I've had more time flexing that muscle than most and I'm also a savage inside, I want to thrive so fucking bad that I

184

feed that savage every day, I let her free to gorge as much as she likes. She is wild and free, and she comes out whenever I need her. However, I can honestly tell you, you have the strength you need, you are a strong person and whilst I write this book, so you don't have to endure what I have, you have that savage inside of you too and she will help you experience what you have to and what you are meant to if you just feed her and let her free.

This might sound strange, but I believe I was meant to go through that much shit so I can do what I do now and I believe I attracted it all for the very same reason.

I want to tell you something else I've learned, just because you're strong doesn't mean you don't need support and it doesn't mean you can't ask for help, it actually makes you stronger, you have to have strength to ask for help when you're strong so go ahead and flex that bloody muscle. I've also learned that even when you don't think you are strong, you will find strength in just asking for help, so go find your strength.

Bottom line is, we are all strong, we all have the strength, and we all have everything we need inside of us we just have to find it. We all have our savage inside of us if we need it enough. I know you have it inside, you know you have it inside you, now it's time to set her free.

I don't know you, yet, but I love you still.

# CHAPTER 26

## MYSELF FIRST

After losing my Nana and my Mum. I developed some of the most destructive insecurities I have ever experienced, never feeling important enough or loved enough. And it was a big problem in my life for years, it was slowly eating me alive. Of course, I didn't realise this at; first, none of us, do. It was only after years of thinking it was everyone else that was the problem and being a victim to it that I finally began to see this pattern, look inside and unpack it. I finally realised I never felt important to anyone because I wasn't making myself important to myself, I didn't love myself.

Sure there was plenty of evidence to support my feelings of never being important enough or loved enough. That insecurity wasn't just born from nothing and the more evidence there was, the less important or loved I felt, the more I felt that way, the more evidence there was, and so the cycle continues. Always looking for proof I was important to someone, that someone valued me enough or loved me enough. Still giving away too much of myself in an attempt to feel it in return. I know you do it also. When we are a victim of this insecurity or mindset, we are in a constant battle within. If I am more, do more, give more, love more, be more understanding, tolerate more, be more accepting, be more willing, be more helpful, and put everyone else first. Then I'll get what I deserve, then I'll be important, I'll get more love and be more loved.

No, guess what? It doesn't fucking work like that. You just stay in a constant cycle of never feeling enough and never feeling loved. It's not because the people around you are evil (well not all of them anyway) It's because you made it so fucking easy for them, you never put yourself first, why would they? You have never made yourself important enough, why would they? You certainly don't love yourself enough, so you will never feel enough love from anyone, whether they were giving it or not. Which in many cases they are not, because they don't have to you will run around trying to please them more anyway right? When you don't love yourself inside and out, and you don't put your needs first and be valuable to yourself, you will always search for that from other people, but it's missing from you, it's inside of you. It is not, and I repeat not something that will ever come from someone else, believe me when I tell you this. It has to come from inside you first, and then it will radiate out to everyone else, and you will attract those people into your life that will operate on that level.

If you don't learn to fall deeply in love with yourself and value yourself, put your needs above all else, you will continue to attract people who just take what you are oh so willing to give and they will only provide the bare minimum in return (or at least that's how it always feels). Because and I know I said it before, but I need to repeat it, you make it so fucking easy. They can only give so much because they can't give more, they don't love themselves either. You accept that because you don't value yourself enough, and they also don't value themselves. They don't make you important, because you don't value yourself enough, and they also don't feel valuable so they can't give that to you. You are two half people operating from the outside in trying to become whole by getting what you need from the other person. It just doesn't fucking work, believe me, I have tried and tried and tried and tried.

I tried so fucking much the cows didn't come home, get it? Ever heard that saying no one can make you happy, you have to be happy first?

Well, it's the same thing, no one can make you feel loved or valuable or enough. You have to be important, you have to be genuinely in love with yourself, and then you will know deep down in the core that you are enough. It all comes from within, and when you make yourself whole, you will almost automatically attract other people who are whole. When you are operating from within, you are sending those messages and vibrations out into the world. Anyone else who isn't vibrating at that level just won't be able to handle it, and they will either do something that repels you, or you will just resist them. Only those who are operating at that level will be drawn to you like a magnet. Just like we attract like-minded people, we also invite the people who are on the same energy level, love and above as I now call it. Love and above is when you are operating from the love you have for yourself first, then the love you have to give. When you are vibrating on this level, your love is so much more powerful, and you can provide it entirely because you never have to worry about getting it back.

If I can inspire or teach you anything from this entire book I so dearly wish it to be this, love yourself, do whatever work is required for you to absolutely and completely love yourself. I want you to unpack whatever baggage you need to to fill yourself up with love, and it might be a lot, trust me it really was for me, and you need to keep unpacking it every day. It might be painful, it will mean you have to really look at yourself and be willing to take responsibility for your part in every unpleasant situation you have been in, but trust me the reward is so delicious. Accept yourself, both the light and the dark, without dark, there is no light. Love yourself unconditionally, completely and joyfully. Be unapologetic with your love for yourself, no one ever says I'm sorry I love you. So don't ever apologise for loving yourself, those who aren't operating on that level will call you selfish, they will say you think you are better than them, they will say think too highly of yourself, they will assume your standards are too high. Bottom line is when other people aren't operating from that level, they will try to tear you down to their level. That's where they are comfortable and believe me it's much less effort to tear you down than it is for them to work on themselves and come up to your level. They aren't bad people, they just aren't your people.

Give yourself permission to do the work needed to love yourself and want what you want. Remember when you had to get a permission slip from your parents to do things in school? Write your own bloody permission slip. I actually mean write one if that is what it takes. Write as many as you need and put them everywhere, so it will continuously remind you until it just becomes second nature. You don't ever need anyone to give you a permission slip, or give you love or to make you feel vital again. Give it all to yourself first, you are the only person that needs to provide you with anything. Put yourself first, set your standards and don't settle for less, make what you want the most important thing to you, learn to fall deeply in love with yourself including all your edges and imperfections and don't ever apologise for it or apologise for being authentically truly you or wanting what you want. You will be happier than you have ever been, you will know deep in your core you are enough, and your people will find you.

This was the best thing I ever did for myself, I gave myself permission, and I learned to fall deeply in love with myself, put myself first and made myself the most critical person in my world. I know deep in my core, I am enough, and it is an unwavering knowing. I'm happier than I have ever been and guess what I have so many people in my life now that just fucking love me for being me. I even have I am enough tattooed on my arm with two love hearts in the infinity shape, that for me symbolises I am enough for me, and I am enough for anyone I give my love to. It also signifies that my love for myself and the love I give, is infinite, it is always flowing in and out, it will always come back to me. It's a constant reminder, just in case I slip, I did tell you it's a daily practice (smile).

Be you, be all of you and love yourself so fucking deeply while you're doing it too. That gave me the most healing I have ever had, give it to yourself also.

I don't know you, yet, but I love you still.

# CHAPTER 27

## AUTHENTIC, DRIVEN AND ALWAYS WINNING

It's no secret among those that know me that I am who I say I am and I show up in this world exactly as I am. I am raw, I am blunt at times, I am intense, I am passionate, I am giving, I am strong, I am authentic, I am driven, and I am always fucking winning (even when I'm not, I really am) but most of all I am loving. I will challenge your ideas, challenge your thoughts and your feelings, challenge how you view Self, and even challenge how you view the world, I will challenge you to your core. But it all comes from a loving place. A strong position fueled by a lot of pain and suffering. With a pure desire to thrive and make a difference.

I see my life as a series of events and lessons that I have endured so that I can share them to help prevent you from making some (psst or all, wouldn't that be amazing) highly unlikely but it's a good thought, right? (giggle)

There are things in this book. I am sure that have shocked you to the core, brought you to tears, inspired you, made you angry and moved you in ways you never expected. I'm also sure some things have made you question me and the world we live in. Good, I want you to feel all of that, not because I want you to feel them for me, I want you to explore them for you. I want you to see yourself in every single one of these events, and I want you to make an internal personal commitment with yourself that you will set your standard for your Self high and you will never waiver from it. I want you to feel deeply, I want you to be so fucking moved you take your life by the balls, and you create whatever your heart desires and do it right fucking now.

I wrote this book to inspire and empower, and I told you the selected series of events for a good reason, it's my way of taking one for the team. All of my mistakes laid bare for you to learn your lessons from, don't learn my lessons, decide what you want from this and learn the lessons that are relevant to you. I want you to see there is so much shit we can endure in our life if we allow it, but we can take so much more than we ever thought possible. There is also so much beauty and love. It's always there waiting for you, you just have to be open to it and look for it. We live in a wondrous world, and we can create our life to be whatever we want it to be, we just have to want it enough. We have to love ourselves deeply enough to give ourselves permission to fly. We don't need to be a victim of our circumstances, we can take ownership of them, own your part in every bit of suffering and own your life every day.

I'm authentic, it's in everything I do, it's who I am deep inside, I actually really like being vulnerable and putting all of myself out there entirely, there is pure beauty in it, and no one can ever hurt you or take it away because when you are truly yourself, and you stand in your power, no one can fuck with that. It's very empowering, liberating and freeing. No mask to hide behind, nothing to hide from, I can't even hide from myself (pure freedom) being comfortable in my own skin, being comfortable with all of me, including the dark and the light (finally). I own my shit, and I walk with my head held high, I am proud of who I have become, I fucking love myself deeply, and I love you deeply too. I am driven to succeed for me, for my family and for you. I'm compelled to share my story and share the lessons I can bring.

I'm driven to create the life I truly want and deserve, and I'm compelled to inspire you to create the life you want and truly deserve. I'm driven to create a movement, I'm compelled to help heal, and I'm driven to make a difference in the world. I'm always winning because I'm still learning and growing and moving forward (I will never stop winning). I'm able to turn around every negative thing in my life, everything, and use it for fuel and power to thrive, and I know you can too.

I hope by now you are starting to see that in you too, go take your world, take back Self, take flight and soar high, smile and rise, smile and rise. Be authentic, driven and always winning (like I know you are)

I love you.

# CHAPTER 28

## DESIRE TO DREAM AND ACHIEVE

I have always been a dreamer as you have learned from reading this book, and I hope you can see that my desire to achieve has always been a driving force for me. Although I didn't always take the right approach, the passion and the intention remained the same. I wanted to create a life worth living, a life full of rich experiences for myself and my children. Throughout my life, I managed to achieve certain levels of success, but I could never break the ceiling. Until I healed myself and learned to fall deeply in love with myself.

At that turning point, my entire life just opened up before my eyes, the sky was now bright blue, even on a cloudy day. The grass was a shade of green I never noticed until then, and I felt peace and joy like never before. Let me share one more thing that was a pivotal element to where I am now and where I am going. Stepping into myself fully, putting myself out there like never before. Being raw and vulnerable and sharing myself and my story with anyone who needs to hear it. Not hiding from myself anymore, not keeping this extraordinary person locked away from everyone, including me. Not being afraid of who I truly am or what I can ultimately bring to the world. Not being afraid to want what I want and to really live life on my terms. Going after what I want, including in my personal life and doing the things I very much desire. More importantly, feeling the way I desire every moment of every day, it is actually scheduled into everything I do.

It is also the reason I finally began to learn to fly, and I do mean fly. I have always had a fascination with small aeroplanes, and I had always wanted to learn to fly. I was afraid deep down, afraid I wouldn't be good at it, so I continued to dream. When I finally got up the courage to try it, it was everything I ever imagined it would be and more. Oh my gosh, the feeling of being in control of an aircraft was just beyond anything I had ever felt. I found out during my first lesson, it was something I was excellent at, it felt so natural to me, and I wasn't afraid anymore. The instructor told me I was a natural, which just confirmed what I was feeling already. I loved it so much I had forgotten anything about being afraid. My first ever lesson and the instructor felt confident enough to let me fly the plane in a straight angle of attack until the aircraft stalled and began to freefall. What a rush of adrenalin and total freedom, I knew right then I had to train for a private pilot licence. I can tell you that the peace of mind and the freedom I feel when I fly isn't like anything else I have ever felt. Only those who fly, know why birds sing. Spending time at the airfield and flying became a big part of my stepping into myself and certainly beats any other form of stress relief I've ever known. I plan to have my own aeroplane and spend as much time as I can flying.

If you have the desire to do something personal that serves you in ways you know will be massive, do it. Do it today, don't let fear hold you back from anything you desire. You will never regret doing it.

Some of these messages may be overlapping themselves, and that is deliberate. It is only through repetition we really learn, and believe me my entire life is a testament to that (giggle). I want these messages to be so ingrained by now, so familiar that it feels like they are part of you. They were always in you, I just need you to remember them. Everything you need is already inside of you, I'm only here to help bring it forward into existence. Set your champion free, she is extraordinary.

I don't know you, yet, but I love you still.

# CHAPTER 29

## MY BUSINESS

### (WHERE IT BEGAN AND WHERE IT IS NOW)

This may be quite a surprise to you considering the complexities of my story at times, but I have had a business life since I left college at eighteen. When I first started my journey in business, I had a business admin service. However, my entrepreneurial spirit and talent were really born much earlier. From the age of ten, in fact, I really began to decide I wanted more from life.

I would do anything to make money, and of course, this is where my cycle of using achievement and drive to drown out anything else that was uncomfortable began. You already know what happened when I was ten. I can now tell you that there is a direct link to me, pushing myself harder to achieve. Each and every time, there was an emotional discomfort in my life. However, I digress, you will, of course, notice the pattern for yourself.

At ten, I would sweep and wash stairs for my Nana and other neighbours who would pay me. I would go to the store for older people who would pay me, help with chores, anything that got me some pocket money. I then started my paper round, I would deliver evening newspapers after school during the week and deliver Sunday newspapers. There was an older girl that lived across the street from me, and she had a much better Sunday round than I did. She also didn't like doing it, so I bought it from her. I was thirteen at that time, my first business purchase (giggle). I paid £53, which was a lot of money back then and roughly what she would have made in six months. I bought this because I knew I could make more money. Her round was in a new estate of private houses, and they were still building more. I knew I could get more customers and grow it, I also knew I would get more tips. Every time new people moved into the new houses, I would go offer to deliver their newspapers. I built it up so much it started to become challenging to handle, and I didn't really enjoy it that much anymore. So I did the sensible thing in business, I sold it (smile).

After my business admin service, I became an aerobics instructor and set up my own classes call Fit 4 Life, I loved it. I would rent out community centres and church halls. It gave me all the freedom I needed with my boys. I decided I wanted more than that, so I went to University to study Law, during that time, I was asked to help an acquaintance with his business, and I became a partner. We worked with less fortunate boys who had been thrown out of school, teaching them to use the discipline from Basketball in everyday life. I was the person responsible for getting the clients and projects. Our partnership didn't go so well despite how well business was going, and we parted ways. I went to all of the clients we had in person and pitched a concept I had for working with girls, and every single client brought me on board.

I put together lessons plans and project outcomes and submitting applications for grants (government funding) that I won. The project was named, guess what? Fit 4 Life, based on the same principles of discipline and respect but teaching beauty and getting these girls back into education. I had eighty-four per cent success rate with that project, and it is something I am immensely proud of. The secret to the success of that project, love and respect. I loved those girls, at the start of every new group I would pick the one with the most attitude (you know the one that looked like she didn't want to be there) or seemed like she would create the most trouble. I would ask her to put her hand out, and when she did, I would motion like I was putting something in her hand. I would say, that is my respect, and I would close her hand. I then said if you chose to keep my respect, I would do everything I can for you and every promise I make I will keep, even if I have to bend over backwards to make it happen. If you don't, I can't help you. Not one of those girls let themselves down. In many cases, I was the first person in their life that held space for them, saw them and heard them clearly. I gave them every bit of my respect because I could see myself in each and every one of them.

Yearning to be seen, longing to be heard and longing to be loved for who they were. I am proud, and I am thankful I was able to give them that for the short six weeks they were with me. Eighty-four per cent of them got back into education and stayed there. I also saved one girl from a drug overdose, her cousin contacted me late one night, she had been missing for two days, we went looking for her and found her in another cousins house slumped in a chair. Called an ambulance and got her to hospital, thankfully they pumped her stomach. I really should not have been involved, it was not part of my role. When she woke up she told me I should have left her there, I shouldn't have saved her, she didn't want to live. She was so angry at me, something I was really prepared for. I told her she could be mad with me for as long as she needed to be, but I was glad I saved her and I would do it over and over again. She cried and hugged me (we both cried) of course. That will stay with me until the day I stop breathing. I couldn't understand how much she must have been through to be feeling that at fifteen years old. I knew her story, but knowing her story doesn't mean I knew her and what she had actually been through.

I travelled back and forth to Beijing to train for massage and after a year of training. I started my salon, Qi it is pronounced Chee, and it means energy in Chinese. I rented a Victorian building over three floors and renovated it all, I put all of my finances into that business, which is actually linked to where a lot of my financial struggles then came from and my decisions to resort to my less than sensible or legal ways of getting money at times. No matter how much I tried, that business just wasn't making a profit. It just wasn't the right location, and it wasn't the right time either. I loved it though, amongst all of the turbulence in my life this was my safe place, it gave me a sense of pride, a sense of achievement. I had the keys to the front door, it was my business, and I had done it all from nothing. Ultimately I had to come to terms with the fact that it wasn't going to work, I couldn't achieve what I wanted.

That was also when we moved away, I put the entire contents of my business and my home into one big van and left the North East for good. We moved to Northamptonshire, and I quickly set about getting my business going again. I began doing hen parties for a party planning company, added treatment packages for hotels in Milton

Keynes and before long, I had a thriving business again. I was well known around the area, and I was very active in the business community. We moved from Northampton to Milton Keynes, and I then opened up a new salon. This is the salon I lost when I went to prison.

After my past caught up with me and I had my little holiday, I set up again in the shopping mall in Milton Keynes. A challenging location, with very high overheads and the added pressure of the community knowing my story. Remember I told you a newspaper was going to print the story, so I gave them an interview first. I ran that salon for 18 months and worked seven days per week, and I just couldn't break even. I had also been living in shared accommodation with my sons to try to make ends meet before moving in with my daughter's father. Finally, the choice to keep fighting to make it work was taken away, four days before my daughter was born, when I received a call from the centre manager telling me they had locked my unit up and I shouldn't come to work. Three days after my daughter was born, her father collected all of my furniture and equipment from the salon. I was devastated, but I had a baby to think about and a collapsed pelvis to recover from.

One year later, I set back up in a space I rented from a well-known health club, it built quickly, and I then moved to a converted barn. It was at that point Manor Grove Spa was born, and the emphasis was very much retreat and relaxation. The business grew fast, and I very quickly outgrew those premises. I moved to a bigger converted barn my landlord at that time had. The company was thriving, and so was I now. This was now when I left my daughters father.

I decided I wanted to launch my skincare brand, I closed the spa. I had already begun with the massage candles within the spa, and I wanted to develop a full range. Elise Marques London was born and still going today.

Now tot he present day, where I run EML and Michelle Margaret Marques Coaching. I have This Woman event, workshops and international speaking engagements. I am working on This Woman foundation and of course, have now finished This Woman book. And there is a whole lot more to come.

I have learned most of all, never ever give up, don't let go of your dreams and desires no matter what. Just keep getting back up, dust yourself off and try another way. Or get up dress up and fucking show up (as I like to say) She is inside you, what are you waiting for? Go fucking get her!

I don't know you, yet, but I love you still.

# CHAPTER 30

## MY MISSION

I cannot begin to tell you how passionate I am about helping other women. Realising that I don't just want to run a business, I want to start a movement has been another pivotal breakthrough. I want to give back in every way possible. It's the very reason I wrote this book, and I am building This Woman mission brand and This Woman Foundation. To help women heal and create the life they really want. To help girls become empowered women. I am committed to providing a welcoming, inclusive and safe environment to celebrate, elevate and hold space for those who identify as women.

A movement where women come together in support of each other, a safe space where we can heal our wounds and co-create our dreams. A place where we are not available for limits or fears. I have seen firsthand the magic that happens when women really come together to share knowledge, support, understanding, care, skills and passions. It is profoundly transformative, and my biggest hope is that This Woman. Becomes a place where you can return time after time to connect deeply with yourself and others in this meaningful way.

I aspire for this to be a space for you to be seen, heard, loved and acknowledged in the complexities of who you are. To learn tangible skills, gain valuable knowledge and to build lasting relationships that grow into business partnerships, mentorships and life-long friendships. I intend to help women who want to create the life they absolutely wish to, women who want to truly thrive. Building your life based on your desired feelings and living exactly as you want to feel each day.

I am on a mission to pay forward inspiration, wisdom and knowledge to more than 1 million women around the globe. Inspiring them to heal, take back Self and create the life they truly want.

A portion of profits is going to This Woman Foundation that will support projects that help women and girls. My biggest goal is to help women create the life they want and stop sexual abuse, child abuse and child marriage.

I am one hundred per cent behind this movement to reach as many women as possible. Through collective reach, and I need your help too. Every book sold has the potential to change lives. I would like to invite each Woman that reads it to write a personal note to the next Woman she is going to give it to. Imagine the ripple effect we can co-create together when you buy just one book. Imagine the possibilities when you buy two or three (WOW).

This Woman isn't just me, it is each and every one of us. This Woman is whoever you want to be. Come join the movement and let's co-create your very own version of This Woman. Be authentically you, driven and always winning.

I don't know you, yet, but I love you still.

# CHAPTER 31

## DELICIOUS DISCOVERY YEAR

I cannot even begin to express or impress upon you thoroughly what an adventure CC and I have had this year so far. And it's not even over as I sit here writing this chapter. In January 2019 I made the decision that this was going to be our best year yet, we were going to go on a big adventure. CC and I came up with the idea of a delicious discovery year, and I can say for sure it has most certainly been that. We left the UK on February 14th valentines day. This was deliberate a very bold act of love for ourselves.

We travelled to New York and spent three months staying there. I've been visiting New York for seventeen years, and I have a severe love affair with that city. I had always dreamed of moving to NYC, and I wanted to finally find out if my New York dream was real or viable. The plan was to spend three months deciding if it was the right move for us permanently. It wasn't all plain sailing; however, we enjoyed the ride as much as possible anyway. Living in New York was a dream come true for me, I love the atmosphere, the energy, the people and the buildings. CC was having a different experience, while there are many aspects of NYC she loves especially the buildings. The business and the hustle and bustle was not something she enjoyed at all. We spent time living in different areas, upstate NY, New Jersey, in the heart of Manhatten and in Forest Hills Queens, which became our favourite. We really enjoyed the uniqueness of the area. The convenience of the stores, restaurants and cafes and the ease of getting in and out of the city. We met some fantastic characters along the way and experienced heartfelt and warm human kindness. Ultimately we decided New York was great to visit and a tempory hub we will always go back to, but not a permanent home.

We moved on to British Columbia in Canada where we will still be before you get your hands on this book. The plan remained the same, spend some time here experiencing life. We both immediately loved it, the scenery is just stunning, and the lifestyle is definitely more our pace. We have bonded with my family out here and had some fantastic adventures. Our visit to Whistler being our absolute favourite. It has given me a grounded place in which to finish my book. The people we have met and bonded with here will always be a beautiful part of our life. Although we initially felt very positive about setting down roots here and making BC our home, we are undecided. However, we plan on visiting here often and are looking forward to enjoying the remaining time we have this visit. BC has a lot to offer mountains, lakes, beaches and breathtaking scenery. It's also very close to the US border, which has allowed me to do some speaking in Seattle and promote This Woman.

We are now making plans and arrangements to move on to the next adventure of our delicious discovery year. By the time you read this, we will be in Barbados. I know I'm so excited, this year just keeps getting better and better. I have been visiting Barbados for fifteen years, and I have friends there. I consider family. In fact, I actually call my friend Herman my brother. I have a special connection with Barbados and always felt it was my second home.

As you know, my wedding to my daughter's father was also there. I have always planned to have a home there one day, even from my first ever visit. I just fell in love with the island and its people. I love the atmosphere and the emphasis on family. What is not to love about hot sunny weather, white sandy beaches and crystal clear blue ocean. Barbados is way more than that though, its a very nurturing place for me and I've never experienced the kind of peace I have there, anywhere else. CC's father is also Bajan, and I want her to experience that part of her background.

As we prepare for more adventures in our delicious discovery year. I would like you to think about what adventures you can plan for your own delicious discovery year. Make every year a delicious discovery year, expect the things you desire most and make them happen. Create the life you want, believe me, it is absolutely possible. If you can dream it, you can believe it, and if you believe it, it's already yours beautiful.

Oh, and you will just have to buy the next book. Or work with me in person, attend a workshop, event or online course to find out about our Barbados adventure. What we decide at the end of our first delicious discovery year and what we plan for our next one (smile). Maybe we will even meet you on your next adventure.

I don't know you, yet, but I love you still.

# Chapter 32

## My vision for the future

### (Notes To My Future Self)

Oh, this is both so simple and sophisticated at the same time. My central vision is to continue to create delicious discovery years with my daughter. Follow my desires and how I want to feel every day. Live my life in my core feelings, love, joy, powerful, free, connection, vibrant and balanced. Travel is at the centre of my world, and I will also continue to fly. I will purchase my own aeroplane so that I can fly and feel free whenever I desire. I will build connected relationships, including a romantic one (it's time, smile). I will have homes in various locations so that I can always entertain and have the experience of coming home whenever I travel. I will create beautiful experiences for myself and the ones I love.

I will continue my movement, build my mission brand and my foundation. I will develop my coaching practice. I will develop This woman methodology, events, workshops, courses, programs, masterminds, retreats and other books.

I will continue to develop Elise Marques London with more products and a home and lifestyle range. A children's range named Elise, and a men's range called Marques Men. I also plan to set up salons, day spa's, hotel and spas and health clubs.

Most of all, I will continue to provide a safe space for women to heal and help you all to create the life you truly deserve. I will continue to be This Woman, authentically me, driven and always fucking winning.

Here's to your future and you being authentically you, driven and always fucking winning. Take back Self, use your suffering as fuel to thrive and create the life you really want, and I will meet you along the way.

This Woman, I don't know you, yet, but I love you still.

Love and Possibilities Always

Michelle xx

# THANK YOU

I want to thank every single person who is or has been part of my life. You have made the ride intense in one way or another, and I wouldn't be This Woman without the experiences you brought with you, positive, negative or neutral. I am thankful for it all, and I give love to you all.

I thank my children for all of the love, joy and tears you have brought into my life and for experiences we have shared, and will share. You are my heart, my soul and my life, and it fills me with pride to be your mum. My heart is full of gratitude and joy, and I cannot believe how lucky I am to have given birth to you all. I love you with all of my heart.

I want to thank Nancy Florance for your beautiful and heartwarming foreword you captured the essence of me and the book remarkably. I also want to thank you for all of your support, encouragement and belief, and for keeping me accountable to myself. Having you read my chapters as I wrote them was an incredible comfort and kept me going when it felt too painful. I love you.

# ACKNOWLEDGEMENTS

Nancy Florence, for the personal coaching that has helped change my life and your loving friendship. Thank you, I love you.

Kat Legowik, for your support, encouragement, laughs and crazy fantastic friendship. Thank you, I love you.

Fabienne Boixel, for your support, encouragement and beautiful friendship. Thank you, I love you.

Karin Ridgers, for your support, encouragement and lovely friendship. Thank you, I love you.

Jennifer Willoughby, for your support, encouragement and continued friendship. Thank you, I love you.

Sam Johnston, for your support, encouragement and great friendship. Thank you, I love you.

Jessica Eriksson, for your support, encouragement and caring friendship. Thank you, I love you.

Rosemary Ann Moffat-Smith, for being a fantastic loving Aunt, and friend. Thank you, I love you.

John Smith, for your support, encouragement, and warm friendship. Thank you, I love you.

John Moffat, for inviting me and CC into your home and welcoming us to Canada. Thank you, I love you.

Kerry and Ryan, for giving me a grounded, peaceful place to finish this book. Thank you, I love you.

Credits:

Rebecca, for your support, encouragement and beautiful cover photograph. I learned so much from our photoshoot in NYC. Thank you, I love you.

Dani, for your fantastic cover design. Thank you, I love you.

Ana, for formating my book. Thank you, I love you.

If I haven't mentioned you here by name, please don't feel left out I'm just tired now (giggle) I appreciate and love you still.

Manufactured by Amazon.ca
Bolton, ON